Improving
People's Lives

Improving People's Lives

Lessons in Empowerment from Asia

Editor
Mukul Sharma

Contributors
Ali Dastgeer
Siti Hawa Ali
Muthuvadivoo Sinnathamby
Gregory Placid

SAGE Publications
New Delhi / Thousand Oaks / London

in association with

THE
COMMONWEALTH
FOUNDATION

London

First published in 2003 by

Sage Publications India Pvt Ltd
B-42, Panchsheel Enclave
New Delhi 110017

<table>
<tr><td>Sage Publications Inc
2455 Teller Road
Thousand Oaks, California 91320</td><td></td><td>Sage Publications Ltd
6 Bonhill Street
London EC2A 4PU</td></tr>
</table>

Published by Tejeshwar Singh for Sage Publications India Pvt Ltd, phototypeset in Aldine 401BT and Futura Bk BT by Krishtel eMaging Solutions Pvt. Ltd., Chennai and printed at Chaman Enterprises, New Delhi.

Library of Congress Cataloging-in-Publication Data

Improving people's lives: lessons in empowerment from Asia / editor, Mukul Sharma; contributors, Ali Dastgeer [et al.].
     p. cm
Includes bibliographical references and index.
     1. Non-governmental organisations—South Asia—Case studies. 2. Non-governmental organisations—Asia, Southeastern—Case studies. 3. Community development—South Asia—Case studies. 4. Community development—Asia, Southeastern—Case studies. 5. Social action—South Asia—Case studies. 6. Social action—Asia, Southeastern—Case studies. I. Sharma, Mukul, journalist. II. Dastgeer, Ali.

HC430.6.I46   361.7′0954—dc21   2003   2003001770

ISBN: 0-7619-9603-6 (US-Pb)   81-7829-228-9 (India-Pb)

Sage Production Team: Abhirami Sriram, D. Srilatha, Mathew P. J and Santosh Rawat

Contents

List of Abbreviations and Acronyms

AKRSP	Aga Khan Rural Support Programme
CO	Community Organisation
CSO	Civil Society Organisation
CSPA	Co-ordinating Secretariat for Plantation Areas
EXCO	Executive Committee
GBTI	Ghazi Barotha Taraqiati Idara
GS	Gram Sevak
HAWA	Women Secretariat
HDI	Human Development Index
HIVOS	Humanistic Institute for Co-operation with Developing Countries
IIZ/DVV	Institute of International Co-operation of the German Adult Education Association
ISA	Internal Security Act
JRY	Jawahar Rozgar Yojana
KAVAL	Kerala Voluntary Agencies League
KILA	Kerala Institute for Local Administration
LSGI	Local Self-governance Institution
MCA	Malayan Chinese Association
MIC	Malayan Indian Congress
MIRJE	Movement for Inter-racial Justice and Equality
NACIWID	National Advisory Council for the Integration of Women in Development
NARESA	Natural Resources, Energy and Science Authority of Sri Lanka
NCWO	National Council of Women's Organisations
NDP	New Development Plan
NEP	New Economic Policy
NGO	Non-governmental Organisation
NIC	National Identity Card
NOVIB	Netherlands Organisation for International Development Co-operation
NRSP	National Rural Support Programme

NWFP	North-West Frontier Province, Pakistan
OSCC	One-stop Crisis Centre
PO	People's Organisation
PRI	Panchayati Raj Institution
RSP	Rural Support Programme
SAP	Structural Adjustment Programme
SAPAP	South Asia Poverty Alleviation Programme
SHG	Self-help Group
SRSC	Sarhad Rural Support Corporation
SSA	Social Scientists' Association
TBA	Trained Birth Attendant
TDFF	Trivandrum District Fishermen's Federation
ToT	Training of Trainers
UMNO	United Malays National Organisation
UN	United Nations
UNDP	United Nations Development Programme
USAID	United States Agency for International Development
VDO	Voluntary Development Organisation
WAO	Women's Aid Organisation
WCC	Women's Centre for Change (formerly Women's Crisis Centre)
WWF	World Wide Fund for Nature

Foreword

This book is the outcome of the Commonwealth Foundation's second NGO Documentation Fellowship programme, which was held in the Asian region from September to December 1999. It is part of a Commonwealth-wide series on the theme of *Lessons in Empowerment*. Having been preceded by a volume from the Caribbean, it will be followed by further volumes from Africa and the South Pacific.

The Foundation is an intergovernmental organisation resourced by and reporting to Commonwealth governments. It works within civil society in the Commonwealth and facilitates connections between people, their associations and communities, so as to encourage mutual learning in the fields of professional and community development. To this end, it initiated an analysis and documentation programme in 1998 with a view to publishing material about the work of NGOs, especially in developing countries, which would be written not by outsiders, but by people working within these organisations.

This annual Documentation Fellowship provides a selected group of four prominent NGO leaders an opportunity for the analysis and documentation of their experiences, the exchange of ideas, and the publication of their stories in a book. The Fellowship has been organised regionally, and the first programme took place in the Caribbean, with participation from Belize, Guyana, Jamaica, and Trinidad and Tobago. The reports of the four Caribbean Fellows on their advocacy and development work were published in April 2000 under the title, *Spitting in the Wind*.

This Asian Volume documents NGO work across a huge geographical area, from Peshawar to Penang. It reflects the diversity of this area in the countries represented—India, Pakistan, Malaysia and Sri Lanka—and draws out important lessons in empowerment for rural communities, community-based organisations, women and ethnic minorities. The Foundation is indebted to the four Fellows for recording their stories, and to the Editor, Mukul Sharma of India, for helping to shape their material.

An important feature of this scheme is that the Foundation seeks publishers within the region of each Fellowship programme. Thus, the Caribbean volume was brought out by Ian Randle Publishers of Jamaica, and the Foundation is now pleased to collaborate with Sage Publications, based in India, to produce this Asian volume.

Colin Ball
Director
The Commonwealth Foundation

Acknowledgements

The Commonwealth Foundation is grateful for the support and collaboration of the four organisations whose work is documented in this book. These are: the Aga Khan Rural Support Programme in Pakistan; Sahayi in Kerala, India; the Satyodaya Centre in Sri Lanka; and the Women's Centre for Change (formerly Women's Crisis Centre) in Penang, Malaysia. It wishes to thank the rural communities, the village and community-based organisations and the many individuals who co-operated in the research undertaken by the authors.

The Foundation is indebted to the Aga Khan Rural Support Programme and Sahayi for each allowing a member staff (Ali Dastgeer and Gregory Placid) to participate in the Fellowship programme, and also to the University of Peradeniya and the Universiti Sains Malaysia respectively for granting leave of absence to the two other authors featured in this book (Muthuvadivoo Sinnathamby and Siti Hawa Ali).

The Foundation also wishes to acknowledge the assistance of the Society for Participatory Research in Asia (PRIA) for helping to organise the first residential meeting of this Asian NGO Documentation Fellowship programme in New Delhi, India in September 1999; and to the Women's Centre for Change for hosting the second residential meeting of the programme in Penang, Malaysia in December 1999.

Series Note

During the period 1999–2003, the Commonwealth Foundation has undertaken to produce a series of four books on the theme 'Lessons in Empowerment'. Each volume of the series includes reports of work undertaken by NGOs in four regions of the Commonwealth: Africa, Asia, the Caribbean and the South Pacific. The reports have all been written by leaders from the NGOs featured, and cover a variety of NGO concerns and activities. Each book is being co-published by a commercial publisher in its region of origin.

Introduction

Mukul Sharma

This is a book about the experiences of four non-governmental organisations (NGOs) and the strategies for empowerment they have developed in select countries of South and South-East Asia. The case studies presented here, of Sri Lanka, Pakistan, India and Malaysia, cover a diverse range of approaches to people's empowerment, from strategies for capacity-building within NGOs to those applied to work with marginalised people. The contributors to this volume have addressed the problem of disempowerment among the rural poor, plantation workers, women and girl children. Their analysis has led them to interrogate dominant development discourses, and to re-examine the position of NGOs vis-à-vis other institutions. They argue that these institutions—including the state, government, bureaucracy and donors—can be renegotiated, regardless of the degree of 'otherness' that they proclaim, to create new relationships that evolve through the processes of relocating them within the programmes of NGOs.

The contributions are self-narratives, as all the contributors have played a part in making this empowerment happen. These are authentic accounts, as the actors here know better than anyone else as to what happened to them in the evolution of their respective NGOs. The contributions are therefore subjective, objective and reflective accounts of their lives and work. The process of preparing this volume has been as important as the product itself. The writers, along with others involved in the making of this volume, met twice—at the beginning in New Delhi, India, where they discussed their subjects, and at the end in Penang, Malaysia, where they reviewed their contributions. In their willingness to discuss experiences frankly, and their readiness to take criticism as good learning opportunities, they sharpened their own

I am thankful to Dr. Rajesh Tandon, President, PRIA, who not only spurred me on to take up the role of an editor, but also sustained me in completing this task through several personal–professional interactions and comments on my drafts. Mr. Colin Ball, Director, Commonwealth Foundation, was very forthright in giving his suggestions, which helped me substantially in reworking my earlier drafts. Dr. Charu Gupta, a modern Indian historian, provided a focus to my whole thinking and writing, invaluably and in several ways. I am also grateful to Prof. Meghnad Desai of the London School of Economics for his comments, amidst his busy schedule. Ms. Diana Bailey has been a supportive presence throughout this exercise. I also remember my friend Amitabh Behar, who always remains with me in these endeavours in one way or another.

voices and, more importantly, began treating each other as both sources and repositories of their learning.

The book deals with concrete programmes of rural development, community organisation, women's empowerment and NGO capacity-building. It describes how NGOs in Asia have evolved their programmes, and delineates their attempts to deal with a range of problems. It addresses a number of questions such as: what variations and common features do the NGOs demonstrate? Are they simply concerned with their specific programmes and their target groups, or do they illustrate some deeper fundamental principles? Are these the ways in which a range of groups within civil society can advance? What are the various tools of conscientisation and empowerment? What, indeed, is the relationship between NGOs and the state?

THE CURRENT VERSION AND VISION OF ASIA

Through the ages, Asia—which comprises more than half of the world's population—has been the heart of the world's civilisation. Asia is extensive and disparate, with widely varying economic and political contexts, and boasts a great degree of variety in geography, culture, socio-political backgrounds and levels of development. It ranges from South Asia, where a large number of people live below the officially stated poverty line, to the 'newly industrialising economies' of South-East Asia, where people live in the midst of a mass consumption era. In economic terms, Asia stretches from Japan, one of the richest countries in the world, to Bangladesh, one of the poorest. It is a region of diverse religious allegiances, where religious identities often come into conflict with each other. Asia spans a wide political spectrum, stretching from democracy to military dictatorship, from veiled authoritarianism to market socialism.

South Asia alone accounts for about a fifth of all humankind, inhabited by well over a billion people. It is a well-defined geographical region, with a shared social, cultural and civilisational past. Its major religions are Hinduism, Buddhism and Islam. The region is packed with people from numerous ethnic backgrounds. Its post-colonial history has been mired in communal and inter-state conflicts, deeply dividing the region. South Asia today stands at the crossroads of hope and despair, having witnessed progress since political independence which has been neither adequate nor equitable. It has emerged as the poorest, most illiterate, most malnourished and least gender-sensitive region. It has the dubious distinction of being home to 515 million of the world's poorest people. It accounts for approximately 80 million malnourished children and as many as 400 million illiterate adults. At the same time, politically, most of the countries in the region represent a vibrant democracy.

In comparison, the countries of South-East Asia have enjoyed a higher and sustained economic growth over the past three decades. These countries have come to be known as the 'Little Tigers of Asia'. Singapore and Malaysia have been transformed into modern economies with an increase in average incomes, combined with comfortable housing and high standards of education and healthcare. Politically, however, the countries of this region are known for the relatively authoritarian nature of their governments. All the countries in the region today are multi-ethnic, multi-religious and multilingual. Most of them have a dominant culture, language and religion. Most of them are also territorially small.

The widely divergent backgrounds and characteristics of Asian countries makes the search for universal solutions complicated. Each country has constructed its own narrative of economic development and political evolution. Yet, despite the diversity in the region, the countries of Asia have not shown much difference in their development approach, and have several commonalities. All of them have been experiencing a uniform process of structural adjustment, liberalisation, free market, setting up of special economic zones and inflow of foreign direct investment. Each country has also opted for a change from agriculture to industry to service in order to boost the economy. Development has become the credo for all of them.

Asia has indeed become the home of triumphant globalism. Globalisation through unrestrained trade and investment liberalisation has become a dominant feature of society. Gone are the days when political leaders like India's Jawaharlal Nehru claimed that Asia had been the source of all important human religions, or when Indonesia's Sukarno, at his famous Bandung Conference, tried to unite Asia with Africa, advocating a new role for the 'coloured' people of the world. These are the days of seeing Asia as a part of the global market, and as the single largest trading community (reflected in organisations like the Asia Pacific Economic Forum, the Pacific Economic Consultative Committee and many others). Asia's very legitimacy seems to be based on the promise of a shared millennium of economic growth and free market economy. We hear increasingly extravagant promises from Deng Xiaping's coarse 'to be rich is glorious' to Singapore's almost achieved goal of a 'Swiss' standard of living, that extract yet more growth and continue with the pursuit of a distinctive political-economic regime.

The economic growth of Asia, or the 'Asia miracle', as the World Bank has termed it, has immensely influenced development theories and practices since 1970. The conditions of macroeconomic and political stability, along with a strong state, were said to be the prime reasons for sustained economic growth and human welfare in the 'miracle' countries. Dazzling figures of growth rates, per capita incomes, infrastructural development and the presumed 'well-being' of the people in the newly industrialised countries of Asia were touted as evidence of the correctness of the neo-classical economic paradigm of development, and it was suggested that other countries in Asia and the developing world should follow suit.

Thus, in a single generation, the economy and polity, as also the technology and individual capabilities, underwent a transformation that was beyond imagination. Since the 1990s, in the ongoing era of globalisation, an added theme of global democratisation through markets has been attached to the dominant economic discourse. It has not been worth considering that many of the political regimes in South-East Asian countries are in fact dictatorial, albeit camouflaged in elaborate fig leaves.

DEVELOPMENT DISCOURSE

The whole discourse of Asian economic development remains homogenised, with a consensus at the top, in spite of having experienced the meltdown from the Asia miracle. It is a flawed model of development and progress, as it measures development only in terms of quantitative indicators and state and corporate interests, and ignores the people's conditions and welfare. It is often forgotten in the euphoria over development that the latter extracts a huge cost and those who pay for the same are those who have little opportunity to defend themselves. When there was a crisis in this developmental discourse and model, the simple argument was that bad loans and negative results of 'cronyism' had transpired because they were not 'visible' and that what was needed was merely better accountability through disclosure rules and the application of internationally accepted standards.

However, there are concrete counter-arguments that are apparent in the contributions to this volume. Economic growth has not proven as beneficial as had been projected. If it has not brought about economic and technological equality between nations, neither has it done so within them. It certainly has not done away with inequality. The current economic growth has actually succeeded in dehumanising society, in a very real and profound sense. Insatiable consumerism has given rise to various social and personal tensions. Many feel more victimised than benefited.[1] The rural poor of Pakistan are one such category of people who have missed out on the benefits of this economic growth. Others include indigenous minorities, such as the Tamil plantation workers of Sri Lanka, who live mostly in the remote areas. While the victimisation process varies from country to country, marginalised people across political and geographical divisions unanimously feel the need for empowerment. All express the need for economic security, fulfilment of basic needs, safety and harmony, social justice and responsive and participatory governance, although the contexts themselves may vary.

Development does not merely imply economic growth or a simple increase in per capita income. Human empowerment does not come about just through the making of cars and computers. The study from Malaysia bears testimony to this statement of fact, revealing how even after a drastic restructuring of the economy, high economic growth rates and the attainment of the status of 'a country in the upper middle income group', Malaysia's women and girl children are still subjected to increasing instances of domestic violence. It is the NGOs that have primarily paid attention to this problem and demonstrated not only that 'development, if not engendered, is endangered', but also that it is more meaningful to talk of development in the wider context. Development must imply not the exclusion but rather the inclusion of marginalised people, their efforts, experiences, dreams and hopes. Development for the NGOs signifies a concern for people rather than projects, and therefore a focus on training, awareness-raising, social organisation, capacity-building and institutional development.

All the studies in this volume question the dominant discourse of development, not just from within the contours of development theory, but from the practical endeavours of organisations that have engaged with people's issues and responses through a long and sustained journey.

While each study has a specific focus by virtue of its subject matter, together the contributions weave a critique of the Asian experience from the perspective of people's empowerment.

COMMUNAL AND ETHNIC DIVIDES

Asia is a witness to many other crises. The tragic costs of violent conflict are eminently evident to all. Communal and ethnic divides and their complex (and often violent) expressions, such as those witnessed in Sri Lanka, have forced us to engage with the issues of culture, tradition, change and autonomy, and to find new ways to promote social organisation and social relations along the borders of nation states.

Relations between different religious and ethnic communities have been considerably disturbed in South Asia in the 1990s. They have been characterised by inequality in power and status, by assertions of superiority, by prejudice, aggression and exploitation. No state in South Asia is free from internal strife. The politics of ethnicity may have roots in the fear of being submerged and of losing one's culture and language, which, in turn, gives rise to ethnic nativism and communalism. Moreover, basic economic issues, the problems of backwardness and demands for development and justice are often used to mobilise people along ethnic, communal and caste lines. The sense of otherness is given a boost in such an atmosphere.

There have been serious attempts to polarise the majority Hindu community in India against the 'Others'—Muslims and Christians—in order to capture state power. A Sinhala-Buddhist chauvinist ethos has been prevalent in Sri Lanka since 1956. The dominance of a military-bureaucratic oligarchy in Pakistan has systematically used Islam to constrain political processes, thereby preventing the emergence of issue-oriented politics and institutionalised grass-roots mobilisation. In Malaysia, the implementation of a 20-year perspective plan—the New Economic Policy—to bridge the income inequalities between the *Bumiputras*, the indigenous Malays, the Chinese, Indians and other Malays—has acknowledged the conflicts and tensions prevalent in the society.

A sense of anxiety and insecurity caused by the loss of land, declining control over resources, displacement and the undermining of culture and autonomy, combined with communal riots and pogroms, have pushed the minorities further into their own world. Many societies are at war among themselves. People belonging to different minorities, ethnic, religious, linguistic and indigenous tribes/communities have been engaged in struggles against the state for the protection and preservation of their social, cultural and economic rights. Communal violence has become so common and mutual mistrust so ingrained, that any kind of broader social mobilisation on development becomes virtually impossible. What is important is not only to say a clear-cut 'no' to communalist and divisive politics, but also to empower people to meet their needs. The need is to highlight similarities and interconnections among communities, while also recognising actual differences and inequalities. A continuum of autonomy, dependence and interrelationship between different ethnic and religious groups, realised through concrete projects, is the need of the hour. Numerous examples of such significant interventions can be found in the case studies presented in this volume.

PEOPLE/SOCIAL CLASSES

Who has created the wealth of Asian countries in the last few decades? It has primarily been the labouring classes—rural and urban labour, toiling women and men. Industrialisation, international competitiveness and the ability to attract investment and capture export markets in these countries has been achieved to a considerable extent, by a reliance on cheap and hard-working labour. As Malaysian Prime Minister Mahathir said in early 1994 in response to criticism of low wages: 'Once we moved into manufacturing and produced the same things they were producing, at a lower price, they seemed to want to take away the only comparative advantage that we have: this low-cost labour. They know very well that if we lose that and we have none of the other comparative advantages, then we will not be in a position to compete'.[2]

But the poor regularly lose out in the wealth creation processes, such as when they find their lands taken over and given up for industry 'in the national interest', or when they are denied their traditional usage of forest area on the grounds that it is a national resource that must henceforth be managed scientifically, or when big dams submerge their most productive valleys, again 'in the national interest', and they receive little or no compensation for the same. In this way, the poor, the disadvantaged, and the marginalised are often sacrificed at the altar of 'growth'.

Persistent poverty, along with vulnerability to industrial and environ-mental hazards, seems to be the fate of a large number of people in Asia. What kinds of organisations have been giving voice to these marginalised sections? What are the alternate means of thinking and practice that have been emerging? Governments often see the labouring people and their organisations not as worthy partners, but in fact as potential threats. Futhermore, it has been a period of new uncertainties in Asia. The trade unions, professional associations, social organisations and charity bodies, to which great energies had been devoted in the 1960s and 1970s, have now become dim lights. There seems to be an exhaustion of visions and dreams as many sections of society have become preoccupied with an interrogation of their past, present and future. Yet, different kinds of organisations have taken root as well. Today, thousands of individuals and groups all over Asia, in spite of various adverse circumstances, are engaged in searching alternative ways for millions of lives. Even if their impact is not all-encompassing, the role of NGOs, community-based organisations at the grass-roots level, new social movements and progressive individuals is difficult to ignore in the present scenario.

NGOs, CIVIL SOCIETY AND THE WORLD OF WORK

NGOs are among the important organisations that have witnessed substantial growth in the recent years. While history is replete with examples of informal action taken to mitigate the suffering of people since the birth of mankind, the growth of formal NGOs is a com-paratively recent phenomenon. Asia, particularly South Asia, has a sizeable number of NGOs that proliferated in the 1980s and the 1990s, fuelled by the increasing needs and demands of the subalterns. The common backdrop against which their growth took place was the grim economic scenario for marginalised people, and the escalating demands for democratic space. NGOs employed a variety of methods to pursue their goals. They protested against and rejected the policies of the state. They tried to alter development discourses by raising serious concerns about the environment and the sustainability of development, about women, about traditional people and their knowledge base, about cultural diversity, and about civil rights, justice and equality. They organised people in pursuit of development, and adopted simple locally relevant, and effective development models. They reflected a mosaic of issues, processes and responses found in different regions.

NGOs have thus endeavoured towards the cause of the under-privileged section of the society, constantly working to enhance the livelihoods of the poor. In recent years, their role has been increasingly preceived as representing a multitude of things. First, there is a notion that NGOs represent a force towards democratic and pluralistic civil society, offering alternative development and empowerment at the grass-roots level. Second, there is a perspective that NGOs possess particular strengths in work related to poverty alleviation and sustainable development.

Third, is the view that they offer the prospect of enhancing the efficiency of public sector service delivery. As Rajesh Tandon, a pioneer in the field of development NGOs, aptly summarises, 'It is important that NGOs are viewed . . . as expressions of autonomous, decentralised initiatives, as manifestations of democratic processes and forms, as non-profit voluntary efforts, as expressions of social commitment for an equitable and just society.'[3]

However, while NGOs in Asia are an integral part of the process of welfare and development and a contributive factor to the process of socio-political change, they are not the decisive element. In fact, their most important role can, at best, be as 'facilitators' of participatory processes, whereby they can ensure, on the one hand, that the government does not absolve itself of its obligations, and on the other, that the poor can be empowered to enhance their livelihoods.[4]

The NGOs in this book had humble beginnings among ordinary people—these include two people in a rented house in Pakistan; a small team of young people in India; a group of women without proper premises in which to operate in Malaysia; and two priests in Sri Lanka. All of them had very modest goals at that time, based on small-scale actions and people's mobilisation. Though they concentrated on the needs of the 'poorest of the poor' in their pursuits they were also demonstrating the important role of a socially conscious middle class.

At the same time, global changes have prompted corresponding changes in the organisation, consciousness and goals of NGOs. These involve, among many things, changes in methods of operation, in the forging of networks and alignment of interests. The access of NGOs to decision makers is greater than ever before, as their advocacy role continues to expand and they are quoted in debates over policy and practice. The case studies in this volume also reveal the new trends among NGOs in Asia, working among the poor, marginalised and vulnerable sections of society. Old liberal visions—such as those of freedom, dignity, justice, equity and human rights—are still basic to their concept of development. However, at the same time, they also look beyond the immediacy and specificity of their own bases. The result is that as civil society actors, they play pragmatic roles, initiating Rural Development Programmes with massive governmental support in Pakistan, and seeking support from bureaucracies to further the cause of women and grass-roots democracy in Malaysia and India. Endowed with more resources than their predecessors, and equipped with infrastructural, managerial and technological capabilities, they have been trying, with a certain measure of success, to play other roles—to link up their activities to networks within and outside of the country, and to share resources, experience and information. This provides a wider and more solid base for NGOs, which is particularly helpful when dealing with complex socio-political systems that allow gradual changes within existing legislative and democratic institutions, yet desist from intruding too deeply on the interests of the ruling classes. Consequently, the case studies here represent a sample of the multiple roles that NGOs are engaged with in Asia today.

The pressing need in Pakistan, for instance, was to address the problems of rural poverty and underdevelopment, without making the false assumption that the benefits of globalisation would automatically trickle down to the rural poor. Measures that would improve the productivity and quality of life for a large number of poor women and men, and that would enable them to continue to live and earn their livelihoods for decades to come, were the need of the hour. The Rural Support Programmes accordingly channelled the willingness and capabilities of the rural poor, and helped them to increase their own incomes. In this programme, village women and men were organised into broad-based community organisations. They were also encouraged to identify their leaders from among themselves. The villagers and the programme then prioritised the problems to be solved, and the opportunities that could be harnessed for the same. The programme arranged the flow of required resources and established linkages between the village communities and the government, as well as with private sector developmental agencies.

In Malaysia, women discovered that joining the paid workforce did not necessarily liberate them. Indeed, there was evidence that the changes associated with economic restructuring were actually aggravating gender inequality and violence. In such a situation, demands for changes in family and gender relations should have been raised widely, but were not. Thus, the Women's Centre for Change emerged in Penang, with an aim to promote a violence-free society through equal and respectful gender relationships among all Malaysians. The organisation focused on women, victims and survivors of domestic violence, and provided immediate services to them. Public education, conscientisation, legal advocacy and research were also undertaken. Engagement with the government, public authorities and the local community was also significant.

The economic policies of the state played a crucial role in the deepening of ethnic conflict in Sri Lanka, where the majority community turned violent against those who were perceived as the 'enemy'. This had obvious negative implications for Tamil plantation workers. They were politically powerless, socially marginalised and economically deprived. Satyodaya established contacts with estate workers and peasants in their own homes and workplaces. Community centres were initiated at workplaces, and health and educational programmes were organised. The Tamil estate worker and Sinhala villager were given opportunities to meet each other. Thereafter, community development activities, through peoples' organisations, have taken precedence over all other programmes.

India has a large number of NGOs and a vibrant civil society. These NGOs are involved in a wide range of activities, and are at different levels of evolution. How they interact—and with what intents, purposes and results—remains an important question. If a particular NGO strives to bring them together through a variety of means, both to develop their skills and champion their broader aims collectively, it would meet a timely need of the hour. That is what Sahayi did through its capacity-building exercises. Sahayi tried to fill gaps prevalent in NGOs, such as a limited information and knowledge base within the organisation; a lack of clarity on both mission and strategy; inadequate training, funding and co-ordination; and leadership problems. Sahayi's services were directed mainly at small- and medium-sized development-oriented voluntary agencies, with a special focus on women's organisations. At a broader level, Sahayi has addressed issues such as passivity among

NGOs towards socio-political and economic issues, the insensitivity of policy makers to the needs of disadvantaged sections, and the low participation of women in decision-making.

The work undertaken by these four organisations is evidence of a search for new methods to address people's needs and defend their interests in Asia. The NGOs here have tried to bridge the gap between different ethnic, religious and gender groups, and have reworked their relationships with the state, private sector and other social organisations. It is important to note that these NGOs did not aim to replace the state in their fields of work. Among them there is an evident priority to meet local needs and to focus on the micro-level, by creating models of popular organisation and involvement. These NGOs also focused on legislative reforms, and skilfully utilised the space created by these reforms to broaden democracy at its base. They have created new institutional capacities within their organisations, aimed at achieving better training, networking, negotiating ability and organisational management. They have also supported the development and grooming of a new generation of organisations and leaders.

One can theorise endlessly on globalisation, poverty and exclusion. The contributions to this volume are concerned less with what globalisation, poverty and exclusion *are* and what effects they have, than with what is required for their undoing, and how the poor, excluded and dispossessed can and should be freed from their poverty, exclusion and dispossession. These are the stories of NGOs that have made successful interventions to such ends. They are also stories of complex and dynamic interactions, and of contest and compromise. Finally, these stories are a pointer to the fact that in order to understand the nature of contemporary Asian politics and society, the experiences and purposes of the region's NGOs also need to be understood.

NOTES AND REFERENCES

1. For an overview of problems of development in Asia, and their impact at the grass-roots level, see Vinod Raina, Aditi Chowdhury and Sumit Chowdhury (eds.), *The Dispossessed: Victims of Development in Asia* (Hong Kong: Arena Press, 1997).
2. Graham Field, *Economic Growth and Political Change in Asia* (London: Macmillan, 1995), p. 26.

3. R. Tandon, *NGO–Government Relations: A Source of Life or a Kiss of Death* (New Delhi: Society for Participatory Research in Asia, 1989), p. 18.

4. For further details on the roles and limitations of NGOs in Asia, see John Farrington, David J. Lewis, S. Satish and Aurea Miclat-Teves (eds.), *Non-Governmental Organizations and the State in Asia* (London: Routledge, 1993).

SELECT BIBLIOGRAPHY

Amin, S. *Delinking: Towards a Polycentric World* (London: Zed Books, 1990).

Anderson, B. *Imagined Communities: Reflections on the Origin and Spread of Nationalism* (London: Verso, 1983).

Arogyaswamy, Bernard. *The Asian Miracle, Myth, and Mirage* (London: Quorum Books, 1998).

Buruma, I. *God's Dust: A Modern Asian Journey* (London: Vintage, 1991).

Chapman, G. P. and **K. M. Baker** (eds.) *The Changing Geography of Asia* (London: Routledge, 1992).

Clark, J. *Democratising Development: The Role of Voluntary Organisations* (London: Earthscan, 1991).

Flynn, Norman. *Miracle to Meltdown in Asia: Business, Government, and Society* (New York: Oxford University Press, 1999).

Gray, J. D. and **D. J. Mearns** (eds.) *Society from the Inside Out: Anthropological Perspectives on the South Asian Household* (New Delhi: Sage Publications, 1989).

Khan, M. Adil. *Economic Development, Poverty Alleviation and Governance: The Asian Experience* (London: Avebury, 1996).

Sachs, W. (ed.) *The Development Dictionary: A Guide to Knowledge as Power* (London: Zed Books, 1990).

Vervoorn, Aat. *Reorient: Change in Asian Societies* (Melbourne: Oxford University Press, 1998).

1

The Rural Support Programmes: Empowering the Rural Poor in Pakistan

Ali Dastgeer

THE BEGINNING OF AN ERA

When the Aga Khan Rural Support Programme (henceforth AKRSP) started operating in the cold winter of 1982 with two people in a rented shop in Gilgit, north Pakistan, few believed that it would be able to provide a replicable model of rural development in Pakistan. But time proved that, in effect, it was the beginning of an era. The AKRSP provided the conceptual framework for the creation of the largest alliance of sister NGOs in South Asia, called the Rural Support Programmes (RSPs). The AKRSP systematically expanded through 'learning by doing'. There were no blueprints to follow. The experiences of the pioneers who had worked in similar projects in Bangladesh and Pakistan provided guidance and the broader principles of community participation, but these were inadequate in the very different geographical, social and political set-up prevalent in north Pakistan. It was the people of the northern areas of Pakistan who made the AKRSP the globally acclaimed success story that it eventually became.

The AKRSP as an organisation, and as an approach to development, was the result of the convergence of several disparate elements. First, the people of the northern areas wanted economic development opportunities, so the Aga Khan Foundation undertook measures to incorporate rural development in its mandate. At that time, the construction of the Karakorum Highway, linking northern Pakistan to China, was nearing completion. As lessons from previous approaches to rural development were being learnt, the Pakistani government was willing to allow a private organisation to undertake rural development in the strategic northern areas. Further, the international donor community had agreed to support innovative approaches to rural development. And finally, the responsibility for implementing the AKRSP's agenda was assigned to the visionary Shoaib Sultan Khan, who was later responsible for implementing the model throughout Pakistan and other parts of South Asia.

The AKRSP is derived from the Raiffeisen co-operative model, developed by Friedrich Wilheim Raiffeisen (1818–1888) who founded the co-operative movement in Germany. It was Raiffeisen who for-mulated the basic principles that guide all co-operatives even today: self-help, self-responsibility and self-administration. Today, these three Raiffeisenian principles propel 640,000 co-operatives in 100 countries with about 350 million members[1].

The liberalisation of the peasantry in Germany and the onset of industrialisation at the end of the 19th century had given the majority of the population, especially those in rural areas, a hitherto unprecedented personal autonomy and economic freedom. Totally inexperienced in managing their own economic affairs, they were soon victimised by unscrupulous middlemen and moneylenders. As a result, many lost their newly acquired lands and were reduced to poverty. Moved by the sufferings and the misery of the rural poor, Raiffeisen—a contemporary of Karl Marx who nevertheless had a different perspective on the devel-opment of society—founded the first co-operative, called the 'Society for Bread and Grain Supply' in the winter of 1846–47 that was blighted by widespread food shortage and starvation.

Raiffeisen was the mayor of the Weyerbusch district in the West-erwald region of Germany. Subsequently, he founded other self-help organisations, such as the 'Aid Society' and the 'Benevolent Society'. He also realised that social work was inadequate and that the focus had to be on empowerment. According to Raiffeisen, this could be achieved only through self-help and self-responsibility. These, in turn, could be sustained only if the economic foundations of the members were strengthened.

The AKRSP today stands on very solid ground. Winning the trust, confidence and hearts of the people has been the most gratifying achievement of the programme. With vibrant village organisations func-tioning all over Pakistan's northern regions, people have been able to double their per capita incomes within a decade with the help of the diverse and need-based economic packages of the AKRSP, ranging from investment in village-based physical infrastructure to the joint management of forests and high pastures.

The AKRSP covers an area of 74,200 sq km and works with a scat-tered population of about 1 million. The social capital of the AKRSP is constituted by 3,557 village organisations with a total membership of 147,467. A third of these members are women. The AKRSP uses the introduction of intermediate technology as the means of developing a synergy between the needs of the communities, their capacity and technology. In this way, villagers have initiated over 2,300 infrastructure projects with the support of the AKRSP. Farm-based agricultural interventions to support sustainable livelihoods have been complemented by the creation of income-generating opportunities in both farm and off-farm sectors through credit and training programmes. As many as 600,000 loans, totalling about Rs 1,560 million (US$ 27 million), have been provided to members of village organisations for investment in natural resource management and medium-scale enterprise development. As a result, these communities have generated a local pooled capital worth Rs 424 million (US$ 7 million) through individual and collective savings.

EMERGENCE OF THE RSPS AND TAKING THE APPROACH TO SCALE

By the year 2000, there were seven RSPs in Pakistan, covering just over half of Pakistan's 124 districts[2]. The Sarhad Rural Support Corporation (SRSC), which operates in Sarhad, or the North-West Frontier Province (NWFP) was the first attempt at replication of the AKRSP model. The Pakistani government's interest in the SRSC goes back to 1987, when it entered into discussions with the Aga Khan Foundation and the USAID Pakistan Mission after a visit by the then Chief Minister of the North-West Frontier Province to the AKRSP. In 1989, USAID appointed consultants at the request of the government to prepare a feasibility and funding proposal for the SRSC. Soon after, the government and the USAID agreed upon the composition of the first Board of Directors of the SRSC, with the former agreeing to provide the SRSC with the service of a government officer nominated by the Board of the SRSC as the new programme's first Chief Executive. The government subsequently nominated two representatives to the SRSC Board, including the Additional Chief Secretary, who would be vested with the overall responsibility for planning and development in the Province. In 1992, the SRSC became the first NGO in Pakistan to be selected by the government as its implementation partner in a large-scale rural development project. This partnership was the first of many that the RSPs would share with the government. In addition to the Pakistani government, the SRSC is also funded by the Dutch government and a Dutch NGO called Netherlands Organisation for International Development Co-operation (NOVIB).

In 1992, the third RSP, the National Rural Support Programme (NRSP), began its operations with core funding from the Pakistani government. At that time, the government had promised the NRSP Rs 1 billion (US$ 19 million) per year for the next five years, with the aim that NRSP would add on 16 districts to its area of operations annually. However, after the first instalment of Rs 500 million (US$ 9.5 million), a change in government meant that further funding was stopped. Thereafter the NRSP decided to place the amount of Rs 500 million in government securities, and has sustained its operations till date largely out of the interest earnings from this principal amount. This method of sustaining operations might have been without precedent in the world of NGOs but, as will be discussed later, it provided future RSPs with a mechanism not only for securing funds from the government, but also being able to operate without governmental interference. With its head office in the capital city of Islamabad, the NRSP is the only RSP that does not confine itself to any one of the four provinces. Instead, it has nationwide coverage and currently operates in 30 districts. The organisation works closely with the government and has also assisted the government in implementing three large-scale rural development projects. To implement its credit operations, in 1997, the organisation secured a credit line of Rs 2.5 billion (US$ 47 million) from a major national commercial bank. Its donors include the Pakistani and British governments and the United Nations Development Programme (UNDP), amongst others.

The NRSP also helped establish the fourth RSP, the Ghazi Barotha Taraqiati Idara (GBTI), which operates at the junction of Pakistan's two largest provinces, the North-West Frontier Province and the Punjab. Initially a part of the NRSP, the GBTI later became an autonomous programme. It was established to rehabilitate all those affected by the Ghazi Barotha Dam, a major hydroelectric project of the government that had displaced around 19,000 people. Among other things, the GBTI helps such people secure compensation for their land and also educates them about environmental issues.

By the early 1990s, the Rural Support Programmes had caught the attention of foreign governments, and the UNDP funded the establishment of similar projects in six South Asian countries under its South Asia Poverty Alleviation Programme (SAPAP). The SAPAP was founded in 1994 as a result of the Dhaka Declaration, issued by the heads of government of the seven South Asian countries, in 1993, wherein they had committed themselves to eradicating poverty within the next 10 years. The Pakistani chapter operates in the Kohat district. It is expected that these pilot projects will develop into nationally replicable models, as is already happening in Pakistan and Nepal.

In early 1997, the chief minister of the Punjab province sought NRSP's assistance in the establishment of a similar project in Punjab. The Punjab government provided the Punjab Rural Support Programme with Rs 500 million (US$ 9.5 million) as an endowment fund. This Programme currently works in 19 districts. Together, these six RSPs have fostered a network of nearly 34,221 community organisations throughout Pakistan, with a total membership of over half a million households. Members of these organisations have accumulated savings of around US$ 14.5 million. Credit amounting to Rs 6.5 billion (US$ 113 million) has been disbursed and villagers have initiated as many as 13,613 physical infrastructure projects costing Rs 2.2 billion and benefiting 566,173 households[3].

HOW DO THE RSPS WORK?

The working methodology of the Rural Support Programmes is very simple. The RSPs believe that the rural poor are willing and capable of helping themselves to enhance the quality of their lives and increase their incomes. However, they need assistance to harness this potential. This assistance, termed social guidance, is provided by the RSPs.

Social guidance includes the following steps:

- Villagers are organised into broad-based community organisations (COs). This is done so that when they start implementing activities to overcome their problems, the villagers can effectively pool resources, cut down overheads and achieve economies of scale. A CO also serves as a guarantor in case credit is provided, through it, to its members.
- The RSP assists villagers in identifying capable men and women from the community to assume management and leadership positions within the COs. Unless these activists, as they are termed, are identified and trained, the villagers will always depend upon external guidance to harness their own potential.

- The villagers and the RSP identify and prioritise the opportunities that the former are ready to exploit or the problems
  they are ready to solve. These opportunities and problems may
  relate to individual households, to a group of households, or to
  the entire village.

- Feasibility studies are then undertaken, concentrating on
  identified opportunities and needs in terms of people's capacity, willingness, equity, sustainability and requirement of
  resources, along with the availability or non-availability of such
  resources.

- The RSP arranges the flow of required financial or technical
  resources to the community. It also establishes linkages
  between village communities and government or other private-
  sector development agencies.

The RSPs believe that the process of constructing a group identity, of
raising consciousness, of acquiring new skills and of upgrading their
knowledge base progressively imparts to the poor a new power over the
economic and social forces that fashion their daily lives. It is through this
power that the poor shift out of the perception of being passive victims
of the process that perpetuates their poverty. Instead, they become the
active force in initiating interventions that progressively improve their
economic and social conditions, and help overcome poverty.

At the same time, the acquisition of power to break the vicious circle
of poverty is based on participation within an organisation. This participation is not through 'representatives' who act on their behalf, but, in
fact, calls for the actual involvement of each member of the organisation
in project identification, formulation, implementation and evaluation.
It is in the open meetings of ordinary members in the village-level
organisations that such decisions are taken collectively and work responsibilities assigned, on issues such as income-generation projects, savings
funds, conservation practices in land use, infrastructure, construction
and asset creation.

The RSPs' participatory management and development efforts constituted an approach which not only gave local people a right to maintain
their livelihood, but also assisted them in developing the capacity to
analyse situations, find solutions and produce responses to key issues
and, in this way, participate in the village-based management and development process. Indeed, the villagers had come a long way from the

token and rhetorical form of development which had hitherto been widely practised and which usually involved simply informing people of top-down directives or casually engaging them in management activities through paid labour.

THE EXTERNAL ENVIRONMENT IN WHICH RSPs WORK

In the five decades since its creation, Pakistan has experienced many upheavals in political and economic development. On the political front, the country has seen frequent changes in government, including three periods of martial law. Since 1985, there have been 14 governments in as many years.

In the 1960s, 19 million Pakistanis were reported to be living below the poverty line (i.e., earning less than US$ 1 per day). By the 1970s, the official figure for absolute poverty had risen to 34 million. By 1995, estimates suggested that there were 42 million 'absolutely poor' people in Pakistan. According to the report entitled *Profile of Poverty in Pakistan*, published by the Dr Mahbub-ul-Haq Centre for Human Development, two out of every seven Pakistanis are income-deprived; two out of every seven lack basic health facilities; three out of every five are education-deprived; while two out of every five are denied employment opportunities. Nearly 62 per cent of the country's adult population (or 47 million people above the age of 15) cannot read or write, while 76 per cent of the female adult population are illiterate.

Other statistics are equally dismal. As many as 61 million people (or 45 per cent of the population) have no access to safe drinking water, and 54 million people (40 per cent) have no access to basic health services. Eight million children are denied education and nine million children under 5 years of age are malnourished.

The 1990s were years of continued slow growth, high inflation, rising unemployment and deteriorating social services. Roughly 30 per cent of Pakistan's population are classified as 'income poor', whereas nearly 50 per cent suffer from the deprivation of basic opportunities of life. Pakistan's economic fortunes and planning have largely been controlled by a narrow group of industrialists, agriculturists, politicians and civil and military bureaucrats. Regardless of political regimes, Pakistan's economy has been dominated by five sectors: agriculture, manufacturing, foreign remittances, foreign aid and a large and vibrant black economy[4].

It is within this context that the RSPs of Pakistan operate. Many villages in which the RSPs work are characterised by extreme weather conditions, remote geographical locations, scattered populations across many small and distant villages, rudimentary physical and social infrastructure, underdeveloped markets and inadequate investments in financial and human capital. Many schools within villages are merely 'ghost' schools due to the lack of teachers; the same is the case with health centres, government agriculture and livestock services. The major means of livelihood for most households is agriculture in areas where there is very low precipitation, insufficient cultivable land and low land productivity. Off-farm sources of income are limited and entrepreneurial opportunities scarce.

THE BEGINNING OF PARTNERSHIPS BETWEEN VILLAGERS AND RSPS

When I reached the place, within 15 minutes, 30 women had gathered because the *numberdar* of the village had taken the responsibility for arranging the meeting. I started talking with the wife of the *numberdar* and came to know that all the people in this village are farmers and that women work alongside men. They look after the goats, sheep and buffaloes. In this village, five people hold 35 to 50 acres of land, and the remaining farmers hold one to six acres of land. The *numberdar*'s wife said that because of the division of land amongst relatives, the situation was becoming grave, exacerbated by the failure of the cotton crop for the past four years.

At this point, I diverted my attention from her and questioned other women regarding their difficulties. Most of them said they owned small pieces of land and that was their only source of income. The literacy rate in the village was very low, on account of there being no school for boys or girls. No one was employed in any government department. Both men and women work together in the fields to make ends meet, but the situation is worsening day by day. On being asked, 'Have you ever thought of overcoming the problem of poverty?', their answer was negative. When further asked, 'Do you ever sit together to discuss your problems?', they answered again in the negative. I said that they could overcome most of their problems by working together. I told them that they could start a number of income-generating activities. They said that they knew embroidery very well. Then I brought their attention towards savings.

I explained the principles of collective organisation, savings and skill enhancement to them. They agreed with the principles and the objectives of the programme, and selected, by consensus, Zahoor Bibi as president and Bushra as manager, and named their CO Mariam. I told them that it would be safer to keep their savings in a bank because of which they would also earn profit. For opening a bank account, they had to collect Rs 1,000. They said they would collect Rs 1,000 by the next meeting. The women were enthusiastic, which leads me to believe that this will be a good CO.

(From the diary of a RSP social organiser in Vehari, South Punjab)

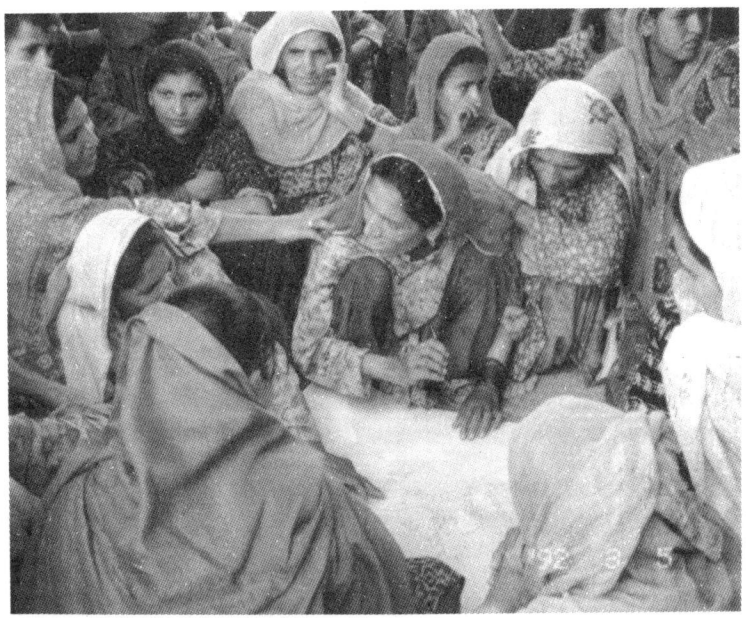

CATERING TO THE NEEDS OF SMALL FARMERS

Zafar Iqbal is just one of the thousands of farmers who have been assisted by the RSPs. He lives in Vehari which lies between Bahawalnagar and the pilgrimage centre of Multan in southern Punjab. He says:

I am 25 years old and live with my family of four brothers and one sister. Two of my brothers have jobs, while the youngest one and I work on the farm. My family owns only an acre of land, but since farming is our main source of livelihood, I had to rent an additional 10 acres of land by selling our buffalo. My other brothers also contributed. Now that I have spent most of my resources on paying the rent, I was worried as to how I would cultivate the wheat in my fields. I could get seed and fertiliser from the dealers on credit, but they would charge double the actual price. Besides this, they would give me products of inferior quality. This is the way in which the dealers and the local moneylenders are exploiting the small farmers. And the small farmers are bound to be exploited because of a lack of resources.

I was in a dilemma when some people approached my village. They told us that they were from a rural support programme. They explained their objectives of elimination of poverty and support to the rural poor in increasing their incomes. I heard the programme with full concentration and felt that these people would help me overcome my problems. However, my neighbours and relatives were not impressed and had doubts about the programme. I tried my best to convince them. Actually, all of them were illiterate and were of the view that these people would commit some sort of fraud, but I managed to convince them and finally they agreed to form a community organisation with 21 members. After the CO was formed, I got a first loan of Rs 17,000 (US$ 321) from the RSP for agri-inputs, which enabled me to apply the agri-inputs of my choice and in time. The second time, I got a loan of Rs 20,000 (US$ 377) for the summer crop. The third time I borrowed Rs 14,000 (US$ 264) for the winter crop. Apart from giving credit, the RSP supported the farmers by arranging 'farmer days' on the seasonal crops, which were very informative. The RSP field staff helped me a lot in this regard. In the regular CO meetings, they talked about crop protection, timely application of pesticides on the crop and other on-farm activities.

At the moment, I am tending a cotton plot that the field staff advised me to sow. I am undergoing training arranged by the RSP on cotton cultivation and protection, which will be completed in three phases. I have laid the cotton plot on one acre and the RSP has helped me use new technology, such as chisel ploughs and ridge planters. By sowing cotton using the ridge planter, water consumption has been reduced by 50 per cent. Thanks to the training, I have applied pesticide at the right time. Earlier, I would apply pesticide to the crop whenever I saw insects on it. The cotton yield in this area had reduced to 340 kg per acre. Now I am fully aware of better crop protection practices and will get the maximum yield from my land.

FROM SERFDOM TO FREEDOM

There are thousands of similar incidents that villagers relate across the length and breadth of Pakistan, and many of these incidents highlight the extreme courage and iron will that people have within themselves to change their destinies. Serfdom is a major problem in many parts of rural Pakistan where feudal landlords have enslaved peasant farmers for generations. Nowhere is the misery of such tenants more obvious than in the southern province of Sindh. Here, in the village of Dani Banjar Khaskhelo, villagers got together to form a CO. None of the members could read or write, so they had to get a young boy to maintain their CO's records. Over time, the members increased their savings to such an extent that they were able to purchase an acre of land to build their own homes, where they now live, free from the fear of eviction. Earlier, they had not even heard of a bank. Today, the manager of their CO, a woman called Rasiti, goes herself to deposit savings. She says that, earlier, they had resigned themselves to a life of slavery and helplessness. Now, they are busy heralding the change in their lives and the womenfolk are actively involved in this.

SELF-HELP INITIATIVES

This spirit of self-help is growing all over the country and countless initiatives undertaken by villagers themselves are being reported. They have repaired dilapidated school buildings, roads and bridges which had suffered neglect for years, paved and brick-lined streets, and pooled funds to instal hand pumps and dig water channels so that they could facilitate irrigation and clean drinking water. Having lobbied with government departments, villagers are now getting telephone lines and electricity installed and are even contributing to the installation of poles and wiring. They have forced the government to reopen and ensure the functioning of the dead village dispensaries and 'ghost' schools. Instead of resorting to the costly, corrupt and inefficient Pakistani legal system, villagers are increasingly solving their intra-village conflicts themselves through the CO forum.

The people of the valley of Nagar in north Pakistan suffered from an acute lack of healthcare and educational facilities, especially among girls. To address these needs, the Naunehal Development Organisation was established by CO members in 1992 with the support of the local RSP.

The Naunehal Development Organisation has since become a highly active local NGO and has received Rs 7.5 million (US$ 142,000) from the World Bank to tackle health and education issues. In the nearby Bar Valley, another NGO called the Bar Valley Development Organisation was established, and comprises seven COs and 265 households. The organisation's most impressive achievement has been Rs 250,000 (US$ 4,717) that it earned from trophy-hunting activities in the area in collaboration with the World Wide Fund for Nature (WWF). The money earned is used exclusively for the development of healthcare and education facilities in the Bar Valley. The organisation has also established an English-medium school and a health centre.

FACING NATURAL DISASTERS

This spirit of self-help and collective effort has also prepared villagers to face natural calamities. In 1998, a devastating cyclone ripped through the province of Sindh and villagers, mobilised by the RSP, played a vital role in helping the victims. While the RSP extended 67 emergency loans amounting to Rs 79,300 (US$ 1,500), the villagers used their savings for internal lending, issuing 19 loans worth Rs 40,000 (US$ 755). Two food camps were arranged for 132 families and eight medical camps provided treatment to as many as 2,216 patients. The villagers also arranged 50 vials of anti-venom serum and 150 bottles of animal vaccine, and contributed Rs 103,753 (US$ 2000) towards relief camps that they organised themselves. In another case, after visiting the RSP, the Christian Welfare Society, which operates in the south-western province of Baluchistan, donated money to COs for building shelters, digging wells and repairing a school building.

DEVELOPING LINKAGES WITH THE GOVERNMENT: ASSISTING IN GOOD GOVERNANCE

The district of Rawalpindi in north Punjab is a classic example of the linkages fostered with the government to initiate, in this case, a drinking water scheme. The managers of five COs interacted with the government's Public Health and Engineering departments in December 1998 in a meeting arranged by the RSP. In this meeting, the villagers raised issues such as the non-functioning of the drinking water supply scheme, and the wrong placement and condition of the pipeline (which was in the centre of the road) amongst other issues. The government officials accepted full responsibility for solving these problems. To run the drinking water scheme on a sustainable basis, the villagers formed a five-member committee which would be responsible for maintaining the scheme (including the transformer and motor), collecting and depositing bills, deciding on water timings and checking and disconnecting illegal connections. In order to carry out these activities, the department transferred Rs 60,000 (US$ 1,150) to the committee's account.

As the instance described above indicates, the RSPs forged strong working linkages between public and private agencies and villagers. Officials from government agriculture research and forestry departments regularly attended CO meetings to provide information on improved practices in farming and agricultural machinery. They also supplied improved varieties of cereal, vegetable seeds and saplings. Other government departments provide training in various skills, held camps and provided guidance in family planning, birth control and healthcare. They extended financial and technical assistance in the establishment of schools and construction of link roads, dams and bridges, drinking water, sanitation, improved small-scale technology, paving of streets and rehabilitation of the handicapped. The livestock and dairy development departments organised livestock camps, in partnership with COs, for the control of epidemics and treatment of animals.

Linkages between villagers and the private corporate sector have also been reinforced. ICI Pakistan, for example, provides medicines and vaccines to CO members. NGOs working in the fields of primary education, adult literacy, family planning, drinking water and sanitation, work closely with RSP-fostered COs, as do many organisations working on enterprise development, enhancement of vocational skills and community uplift.

HELPING VILLAGERS OVERCOME LACK OF CAPITAL

The failure of the formal Pakistani banking sector to provide the poor with access to capital is evident from an incident in 1983, when a meeting of top bankers was held in Gilgit to review the experiences of the government's agricultural credit programme in the northern region. It was discovered that even though there was a directive of the Pakistan Banking Council to disburse up to Rs 6,000 (US$ 113) as interest-free loans to small farmers, not a single loan had been sanctioned in the northern areas from 1980–82. In the Gilgit discussion, it transpired that both the banks and the small farmers had found the arrangement unprofitable due to heavy transaction costs on both sides.

For many poor farmers who need to purchase agricultural inputs such as seeds, fertilisers and pesticides, the RSPs have become a source of easily accessible and timely credit. In fact, the most significant impact that the RSPs have made is in reducing poverty by freeing villagers from the clutches of local moneylenders. Not only do moneylenders force villagers to sell their produce to them at rates determined by the former, they also provide inferior quality inputs such as seeds, fertiliser and pesticides at extortionate prices. An analysis carried out in Lodhran, a small district near Multan, showed that farmers were paying Rs 1,415 (US$ 27) in interest to the local input dealer for the purchase of pesticides. If bought with cash, the same products would cost Rs 2,020 (US$ 38), in addition to which farmers would have to pay the RSP only Rs 202 (US$ 4) as service charge. In Lodhran, the average loan disbursed by the RSPs amounts to Rs 14,556 (US$ 275). If a loan of this size had been taken from the local input dealer, he would have charged at least Rs 10,189 (US$ 192) in interest. But farmers only pay Rs 1,455 (US$ 27) to the RSP, thus saving Rs 8,734 (US$ 165) in each case. In addition, RSP loans are collateral-free; members of a CO take responsibility for each other so that all dues are repaid. This also ensures that the poorest are not denied loans for want of financial assets to pledge.

A survey of 100 farmers was carried out in December 1988 to assess the impact of the RSP's credit programme in the district of Vehari in south Punjab, where farmers borrow chiefly for the procurement of seeds, chemical fertilisers and agricultural chemicals. Results showed that RSP credit enabled the farmers to pay lower interest rates of 20 per cent, as compared to 84 per cent (for the winter crop) and 76 per cent (for the summer crop) they would have had to pay per annum on credit extended by moneylenders. They also showed that with access to capital at reasonable terms, poor farmers and the landless were now able to rent more land, thereby increasing their incomes. The difference between the net return per acre of those borrowing from the RSPs as opposed to those borrowing from other sources was over Rs 1,500 (US$ 28) for the cotton crop and 120 per cent at Rs 2,170 (US$ 41) for the wheat crop.

As much as a third of all RSPs loans are taken by women borrowers. One such borrower, who has done exceptionally well with the assistance she sought, is Zuhra Khatoon, a women's health worker used to live in a hut near Islamabad, along with her husband and five young children until as recently as 1994. She took a loan of Rs 20,000 (US$ 377) and bought a cow and a goat. Each year, her goat had two kids that she raised and sold once they were mature. She also started selling milk. Zuhra was quite successful in her venture and so took further loans to buy more livestock. She also took a loan for the construction of a wheat storage tank.

The wheat storage facility enabled her to store farm produce and sell it later in the market when the price was high. It has not been all smooth sailing, though. One buffalo, which she bought with a loan of Rs 30,000 (US$ 566) in early 1999, fell ill and had to be sold for Rs 11,000 (US$ 208) incurring a loss of Rs 19,000 (US$ 358). At the same time, her husband, who was earning Rs 2,500 (US$ 47) a month from his job, was laid off. Despite these mishaps, she was regular in paying her instalments, which she was able to meet through her salary as a women's health worker.

On the whole though, by 1999, the change in her life was dramatic. Today, if one visits her home, one finds that the mud hut has been replaced by a concrete structure, built from the savings and income she generated through the livestock business. By selling buffaloes and using her savings, she has furnished her house and installed a flush latrine. Other noticeable items in her house include a television, a refrigerator, a washing machine and even a telephone. All these things speak of the rapid strides that Zuhra has made since 1994.

Many villages have also taken loans for building or renovating irrigation channels. In Pakistan's largest but least populated province, Baluchistan, which is characterised by its barren desert topography, villagers have taken RSP loans for the rehabilitation of *karez*, or underground water channels, which are unique to Baluchistan. With the help of these loans, villagers have been able to restore or initiate the provision of water for cattle, drinking water for humans, and irrigation water for the cultivation of wheat, rice, tomato, onion, okra, watermelon, melon and date palms. Many villagers have also taken loans for the installation of engines that pump water from underground tables, thereby irrigating their once-barren lands.

SERVICING THE CASH NEEDS OF THE VULNERABLE

An analysis of a sample of 40,085 CO members from across Pakistan shows the socio-economic classifications of the villagers that the RSPs work with. This indicates that the more vulnerable segments of the rural poor are being targeted and are benefiting tangibly from their partnership with RSPs. Widows, for example, are a sizeable proportion of RSP loanees and there are many examples where they have taken loans to engage in different income-generating activities to support

Figure 1.1

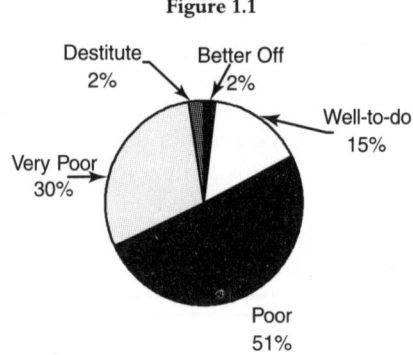

Source: 'Rural Credit and Enterprise Development', *NRSP Sixth Annual Report*, p. 14.

their families such as shopkeeping, embroidery and tailoring, livestock rearing and trading.

Women in Pakistan face great disadvantages. They are burdened with a greater workload than men, are less educated, and have less access to health facilities, remunerative employment and income-generating activities. Women are responsible for most of the unpaid and unrecognised tasks in production and reproduction. Severely bound by cultural constraints and prejudices, rural women of Pakistan lead socially secluded lives. Their mobility, especially in less developed areas, is restricted to the boundaries of their homes. They are largely prevented from taking part in major decisions affecting their homes and communities. RSPs believe that the constraints facing women and the environment in which they live, can be addressed and improved only if women are equipped with tools that will enable them to improve their lives.

Through organising women in COs, rural women have become part of a forum dealing with village development issues. This has given women a chance to discuss issues and to find solutions to these through support from RSPs. Women have successfully taken part in adopting income-generating packages; they have proved to be credit-worthy partners, and have also demonstrated an incredible resolve to tackle their own problems. In certain spheres, they are moving ahead faster than men. In northern Pakistan, for example, savings by women in COs increased in 1998 by 19 per cent as compared to the steady 12–15 per cent by men. Similarly, in the village of Saifullah Qilla in the North-West

Frontier Province, when women were given grants for the installation of hand pumps to access clean drinking water, instead of hiring someone to bore the earth, the women collectively decided to buy a boring machine and saved Rs 170,000 (US$ 3208) for this in partnership with another CO. The machine earns them a profit of Rs 50,000 (US$ 943) a month from hiring out. With this profit, they have opened up a medical store in their village and, in addition, have contracted two doctors to provide medical care there twice a week.

Probably the most inspiring case of this kind is that of Jameela. She lives in the highly conservative Pathan society and says:

My family consists of 12 people, including my parents, six sisters, and four brothers. Two of my brothers, two of my sisters and myself, are all blind. We are a poor family. My father is a retired government servant and we have nearly half an acre of land for cultivation. My younger sister works in a school from where she gets Rs 600 (US$ 11) per month. As you can see, we have very meagre resources to live on.

I felt very inferior to other people. I could not do much to change my family's condition. I often thought that since I was blind I was merely a burden on my family and society. My disability prevented me from attending school. However, because I was interested, my younger sister helped me learn some basic education. I learned counting, could feel time and learned names of different things. I even understand a little bit of Urdu.

One day I got an idea to start a small shop in my home for which I borrowed Rs 100 (US$ 2) from my neighbours. The few things which I put in my shop included packets of salt, matchboxes, soap, candles, peanuts, biscuits, and sweets for children. After one month, I was able to pay back the loan. However, once again I was short of capital.

Luckily, the RSPs helped the formation of a community organisation in a nearby village. I got information about the programme and approached the RSP's women staff through my brother's friend. The RSP staff came and told us about the programme. I was very happy to hear about the programme because I thought that it could provide me with an opportunity to overcome my financial problems. I would be able to run my business again and would prove to be successful despite being blind.

Other women of my village were also interested. In May 1999, we formed a CO in our village with 17 members. I started savings by depositing Rs 10 (US$ 0.2). I requested credit through my CO but had no money to deposit as collateral. The RSP staff helped us and appraised my case. I was able to get Rs 6,000 (US$ 113) collateral-free credit. I bought stock for my shop. My father helps me in getting supplies from the main market. I can feel the currency and manage the sales. The size of my business has now increased. Now I have got all consumer goods used in the village. I got Rs 200 (US$ 4) net profit within a week after obtaining credit. I felt very proud. For the first time in my life, I gave Rs 150 (US$ 3) to my father for use in household expenses and saved Rs 50 (US$ 1) for depositing as savings in the CO. My father is very proud of me.

REDUCING DEPENDENCY ON EXTERNAL CREDIT SOURCES

Lending from their own savings as a means of servicing their needs while at the same time ensuring maximum returns on saving, is an increasing trend amongst villagers with whom the RSPs work. For example, in Kashmir 100 community organisations are currently practising internal lending and revolving funds worth Rs 2.5 million (US$ 47,200). By the middle of 1999, 64 COs had internally lent Rs 677,900 (US$ 12,800) to 146 members in southern Sindh, largely for agri-inputs and livestock. Credit has also been given for illnesses and for education. In western Punjab, when the crop of Dera Chanrawala village was devastated by a hailstorm, the entire village borrowed Rs 150,000 (US$ 2,830) from a neighbouring CO, Mubarak Khail, in order to repay the agriculture inputs loan taken from the RSP. In the district of Kohat, a women's CO lent Rs 30,000 (US$ 566) to a man from the village and earned Rs 5,000 (US$ 94) on this loan in a period of six months. In many COs of the Northern Areas, which are 15–18 years old, savings per CO have exceeded Rs 10 million (US$ 190,000). Such villagers no longer borrow from the RSP and instead practise internal lending.

The majority of the COs working with RSPs around Islamabad are involved in internal lending. One such case is that of Taj Bibi's CO. Taj Bibi is a poor villager from Bhumlehri and her family consists of four people. She has an adult son who is blind. Her husband is ill and has been bedridden for the last four years. Their only source of income is the Rs 900 (US$ 17) pension that her husband receives—an amount that is barely enough to make both ends meet. When Taj Bibi's house was washed away by floods, she approached the community organisation for help. After deliberations, the villagers decided they would provide financial help out of their own savings, and keeping in mind that Taj Bibi came from a very poor family, it was decided that a surcharge would not be levied. Hence Rs 4,000 (US$ 75) was loaned to her, which somewhat helped the distressed woman.

DEVELOPING ENTREPRENEURIAL CAPACITIES

A major activity undertaken as part of enterprise support by the RSPs is the provision of vocational and business management-related training programmes for both men and women, and these will be discussed in greater length elsewhere in the chapter. In the older RSPs, other activities through which business initiatives are supported include technical advisory services, market research, building linkages between local entrepreneurs and town markets, and introducing new ideas and appropriate technologies while targeting those small-scale ventures which have the largest potential for value addition, growth output, and employment creation in the area.

In the remote northern areas of Pakistan, because of their isolated geographical location and the limited size of internal markets, both import substitution and export promotion have to figure in any enterprise initiative which is to succeed in promoting economic prosperity in the area. Keeping this in mind, enterprise projects supported there over the last two years have been in areas of food processing, fruit and vegetable preservation, carpet weaving, wool processing, furniture and carpentry production, and block making. In addition, fruit and vegetable exhibitions and Sunday markets are organised to promote marketing of fresh farm-based products in town areas. Enterprise-related training courses organised during the last year have been in diverse fields, ranging from tailoring and pulp making for women, to gold extraction and wood carving techniques for men.

Apart from traditional, small-scale enterprise-promotion activities, over the last couple of years the RSPs have been contemplating developing larger businesses which have the potential of providing substantial economic benefits for the communities of the northern areas of Pakistan. A seed development company has already been established to promote the production of high quality vegetable seed on a large scale. By the year 2000, this company produced 252 metric tons of certified potato seed, 18 metric tons of carrot seed, and four metric tons of onion seed. The projected revenue generation from the sale of these products is more than Rs 18 million (US$ 340,000), of which Rs 11 million (US$ 208,000) will go to local farmers.

Developing coal mines is another project for which preliminary feasibilities have been completed. Geological surveys of certain valleys in the northern areas have confirmed the presence of enough coal to meet the fuel requirements of the entire local area for the next two hundred years. Laboratory tests indicate the quality of the coal reverses in the valley is among the best in Pakistan. An environment impact assessment of the project is expected to be undertaken soon. The project has the potential of having a substantial impact on the local economy through employment creation, household-level savings on fuel consumption, and a reduction in the workload of women.

The third large-scale project being undertaken by the RSPs in northern Pakistan is for wool processing. This project, termed *Shubinak*, was initiated in late 1997 to create a network of traditional cottage craftworkers. It has grown into a business that protects and develops the interests of village women, maximises their cash income, and keeps the control of production in their hands. In the local language of this northern-most part of the North-West Frontier Province, the word *Shubinak* has two meanings. One is to describe the warping of a loom by women spinners; the other is the local word for spiders, nature's master weavers. Women spinners in these villages spin yarn so fine that village weavers can weave it into light windproof fabric called *shu*. In the past, most *shu* lengths left the villages and most value adding was done elsewhere. *Shubinak* has established women's quality circles in 10 villages; it has also developed a quality control system and village training facility in association with these craft groups. The results have been simple and direct—a return to the high production standards of the past, and a 40 per cent increase in direct cash income for CO members. The project has created a range of 11 garments using a combination of local and classic western designs. These have received enthusiastic initial market reviews, and are now being test marketed in the US and Europe. While *Shubinak* is an outstanding illustration of tailoring centres established with the assistance of the RSPs, it is but one of numerous examples. In Charsadda, lying in the centre of the North-West Frontier Province, a tailoring centre established in May 1988 by CO member Mohammed Din Gul has linkages with a dealer in the provincial capital, Peshawar, whereby the dealer provides material to the centre and buys the finished products. The centre not only trains

CO members in sewing, it currently sews 30 waistcoats a day and is willing to assist the RSP in providing sewing expertise to villagers in other areas. Nearby, in a women's CO called Sherin Abad, a vocational centre established by the villagers has trained 35 women who are earning an average of Rs 400 (US$ 7.5) per month and contributing part of their incomes to sustain the embroidery centre.

These places are the most conservative in the world when it comes to allowing women to interact with people beyond their immediate family. However, the RSPs are working with both men and women to change attitudes. This involves training for RSP staff, government staff, and villagers in gender issues. And change is occurring, as is evident from the case of one woman, Sajida, who comes from a village in the district of Charsadda. She took training in the making of washing powder, candles and flower vases, and then conducted the same training in seven villages. The cost of this training was borne by the village women. At least 10 women have since adopted the skills learnt, and are earning Rs 500 (US$ 9.5) per month. Flower vases, for example, are being marketed in the main towns of the district because of their popularity, especially during wedding ceremonies where friends and relatives offer them as a gift to the bride.

MANAGING NATURAL RESOURCES

The RSPs encourage villagers to enhance the productivity of their lands in a sustainable manner. In order to do this, villagers are exposed to modern farming methods through demonstrations, assisted in procuring improved varieties of seeds, and trained in production and protection techniques. A cadre of specialists is developed at the village-level, which enables these specialists not only to earn a living for themselves but also to benefit other villagers through technical guidance. In the northern parts of Pakistan, where the RSPs have been working the longest, they have started privatising some of their field extension work, with village specialists and master trainers themselves undertaking delivery of services and supplies in their respective communities. Forestry sector activities are one example where the trained community-based forestry specialists are currently undertaking the entire extension work. They own all the forest nurseries and supply plants to the RSP. Other examples include hatcheries and fruit nurseries.

ENHANCING FARM PRODUCTIVITY THROUGH GUIDANCE AND DEMONSTRATION

Demonstration plots are laid out on villagers' lands on a cost-sharing basis which enables other villagers to see the benefits of improved varieties and to adopt them. In the northern parts of Pakistan where, 18 years ago, vegetable growing was virtually non-existent, currently almost all households produce vegetables. Similarly, sunflower promoted by the RSPs in the district of Charsadda has made villagers aware that they can replace the exhaustive and long-duration crop of sugar cane with the less exhaustive sunflower. While sugar cane takes two years to mature, in the same period sunflower can be grown, followed by maize and vegetables. On average, the net income per half an acre of improved variety of sugarcane is Rs 10,000 while from these three crops the net income is Rs 14,700 (Rs 2,500 from maize, Rs 10,000 from vegetables and Rs 2,200 from sunflower). Improved varieties of wheat and maize are also promoted.

The RSPs have supplemented these demonstration trials with strong monitoring systems competent enough to conduct cost-benefit analyses. In addition, RSPs promote improved farming practises, such as the appropriate use of different chemicals in fertiliser, organic farming, line sowing (as compared to broad casting) of seeds, and grafting of plants. This is supplemented with farmers' days which enable the villagers, the RSP staff, and government line departments relating to irrigation, agriculture, livestock and forestry, to discuss problems and share experiences.

ENHANCING FARM PRODUCTIVITY THROUGH IMPROVED TECHNOLOGY

The integrated way in which training, credit, and technical assistance are used as tools to raise agricultural productivity is evident from cases such as Khadim Hussain's, a farmer from Vehari, southern Punjab, who owns six acres of land. He says that he used to cultivate along traditional patterns, having no idea of how much pesticide to apply and when. He recalls there being no one to guide him and others like him, until the RSPs entered the area and he became manager of his village CO.

In the training on cotton production and protection, I learned how and when to use the spraying machines. I also learned how much artificial fertiliser should be used in one acre; previously I applied unlimited quantities. I have also got my soil tested and know what type of fertiliser should be used. Through the RSP's financial support, I bought good quality agri-inputs which not only save my crops from pest attacks but also help in the increase of crop yield. Before, we used to buy a bottle of Methameidophas from the dealer on credit for Rs 425 (US$ 8). Now, in cash, we can purchase the same for Rs 180 (US$ 3).

Farmers in Vehari, on a cost-sharing basis with the RSP, also adopted spraying machines. They are protecting their crops against pest attacks and reporting increases in cotton yields of 60 kg, or Rs 1,500 (US$ 28) per acre.

One of the many technologies that the RSPs promote is 'zero tillage'. This allows farmers to cultivate wheat sooner after the harvesting of the summer crop, thus saving a month due to early sowing and early harvesting. This saves the costs of preparing the land, and surveys carried out in the southern province of Sindh have shown that it also increases yields by around 400 kg per acre.

ENHANCING ACCESS TO CLEAN DRINKING WATER

In the case of drinking-water supply schemes, villagers are responsible for assisting in the survey of the scheme, contributing physically and financially to its completion, and responsible for ensuring it continues to function after it is built. Drinking-water supply schemes also assist in the reduction of waterborne diseases and save women's time in fetching water, often from very long distances. Because of the easier availability of water, many villagers cultivate small vegetable plots whose produce they both consume and sell. In his book, *Government, Communities and Non-Governmental Organisations in Social Sector Delivery* (Ashgate, 1999), Shahrukh Rafi Khan of the Sustainable Development Policy Institute has compared the RSPs' implemented drinking-water supply schemes with others, including those implemented by government. He writes:

Exploring the data to understand why the NRSP schemes were viewed as better managed, we discovered that the quality of construction, masonry, catchment, and better placing and condition of the pipes stood out. With regards to social mobilisation, NRSP communities were better informed, better aware of project rules, and demonstrated more participation and self-reliance. Also, one could view NRSP as being a more demand-responsive project in that communities actually built the schemes, made a greater cash contribution, and indicated a greater willingness to pay for improvements.

In his analysis, the author found the cost of the RSPs' schemes in Azad Kashmir to be 60 per cent lower and in Sindh 15 times lower than those implemented by government line departments.

Other types of physical infrastructure in which the RSPs work with communities include link roads, water channels, dams, and the rehabilitation of land. Over 5,400 such schemes have already been completed in which the RSPs have attempted to create a sense of ownership and responsibility among villagers through involving them in all phases of implementation. The following table shows how the RSP's way of working differs from conventional approaches:

Table 1.1

Government's conventional approach	RSP approach
The line department or politicians decide what needs to be done.	The community identifies and prioritises its need.
The execution of schemes is carried out by line agencies.	The community executes identified schemes.
Surveys of physical infrastructure schemes are carried out by external experts without consulting the community.	Surveys are made in collaboration with the local community, who contribute their knowledge and experience, ensuring a more sustainable design.
The feasibility of a scheme covers only technical aspects.	Along with a technical feasibility study, a social feasibility study is also undertaken to examine the ability of villagers to implement and maintain the scheme on a sustainable basis.
Contractors are responsible for constructing the scheme.	The villagers construct, operate and maintain the scheme themselves.
A number of middlemen are involved in implementation, which increases costs.	This approach is cost-effective as the villagers use indigenous solutions.
The donor agency is not accountable to the community as it has given the scheme in the form of aid or as a grant.	Since the agency signs a Terms of Partnership with the community in which all rights and obligations are detailed, both parties are accountable to one another.

In Pakistan's northern regions, characterised by barren, mountainous terrain, the RSPs have assisted in the building of hundreds of irrigation channels. A cumulative total of 48,000 acres of new land, and 58,000 acres of existing land, had come under cultivation by the end of 1998 as a result. Post-operational maintenance is the complete responsibility of the community[5]. A study of six large irrigation channels revealed that as a result of irrigation channel construction, the average cultivable farm size in the beneficiary villages had increased by 10 canals. It was estimated that as a result of bringing new land under cultivation, the area covered by woodland had increased by 105 per cent, the area covered by orchards by 92 per cent, and area sown with crops by 40 per cent in the villages of the study. In the mid-1980s, an economic cost-benefit study of 154 channels was undertaken, and their average financial rate of return was calculated to be 37 per cent. In most north-eastern parts of Pakistan, the Baltistan region, the farm size had increased from 23.6 canals (as reported in the Agriculture Census) in 1981 to 37 canals[6].

POWER TO THE PEOPLE: VILLAGERS PRODUCING ELECTRICITY

Taking advantage of the free and sustainable power offered by a myriad of fast-falling streams, and by selecting robust, low-cost generating equipment, the RSPs have worked with villagers to install 96 hydropower projects in the northernmost district of Pakistan, Chitral, benefiting 11,000 households. The cost per unit of electricity to Chitrali village households is cheaper than any other known scheme.

A study by Power Flow Limited, a New Zealand group with expertise in micro hydroelectricity, showed that the success rate of such units in Chitral was almost 100 per cent. This was in sharp contrast to very high failure rates on micro hydroelectricity projects in Cambodia and Laos, and a poor showing in Nepal, Sri Lanka and elsewhere in the world. The study attributed the success in Chitral to the attention paid to social organisation by the RSPs, and maintenance and back-up services in the district.

So far, 79 hydroelectricity projects have been completed and are supplying electricity to 8,597 households. The communities are responsible for post-operation and maintenance, and have so far raised Rs 4.4 million (US$ 83,000) in maintenance funds. The communities have also established a system of user charges and penalties, whereby consumers have to pay more for bulbs as they consume more power than tubelights. Households wanting to use fans, televisions, irons, refrigerators, washing machines, butter churners and heaters are also required to pay more.

Such micro hydroelectricity projects have also generated jobs and economic activity. More than 200 jobs have been created at the village level. A total of Rs 208,310 (US$ 3,930) was being paid in salaries to the operators and watchmen of these units every month, and the total user charges in Chitral come to Rs 352,878 (US$ 6,658) each month. A small, micro hydro-shop, which supplies spare parts for the units, has even opened in Chitral town.

The RSP has also provided training to villagers to operate their micro hydroelectricity units. As many as 175 people were given basic training and another six operators were provided with advanced training in the winding of the generators. When one of the operators recently repaired a burnt generator, he was paid Rs 15,000 (US$ 283) for the assignment.

Compared to these micro hydels, a 2.8 megawatt hydel-power project built by the government in the same district in 1988 is still not operational. In contrast, the village in which it was built is already producing 100 kilowatts of electricity from its own unit, which was installed and put into operation in a period of a few months. Women are perhaps the biggest beneficiaries; because they perform certain household chores at odd hours, the availability of light has made a significant difference to their lives. The butter churners run by electricity and have reduced their workload; and the use of washing machines, irons, and fruit dryers has brought them much comfort. Families point out that electricity has enabled their children to study late at night, which was not possible with lanterns using kerosene oil.

Another aspect of this experience in Chitral is the utilisation of local-level expertise. The micro hydroelectricity projects use a minimum number of engineers for supervision, and the RSP operating in the district has only one engineer who supervises the projects. The hydropower projects are handy and simple, and even illiterate villagers find them easy to maintain. Poles carrying electricity wires are made of the abundantly available local wood, and the villagers build a small room to house the generator and machines. Advanced technologies like load controllers and transformers are installed once the villagers get used to the simple system, which manages to meet the basic lighting needs of the communities. Additionally, as many CO members point out, they do not have to bother about the excessive billing, wrong meter-reading, power thefts, power breakdowns or load-shedding that is normal in places supplied by the government's electricity department[7].

INCREASING COMMUNICATION

In the district of Mansehra in the North-West Frontier Province, the villagers of Gorbandi and the RSP contributed finances almost equally to construct a road. The road has enabled the villagers to increase their incomes substantially. There are 140 households in the village, each household consuming an average of 60 kg of flour a month. Before the road was constructed, the villagers used to take the grain to the water mill by hiring a mount, which would cost them Rs 90 (US$ 1.7) for 40 kg. Now, by jeep, it costs them Rs 30 (US$ 0.56). The entire village is thus saving Rs 151,200 (US$ 2,850). The village has a treasury of around 1,000 walnut trees, which produce an average of 80 kg of fruit per tree. Previously, the villagers used to sell the produce to a middleman for Rs 800 (US$ 15) per 40 kg. Now they market it themselves at a rate of Rs 950 (US$ 18) per 40 kg. The village thus makes an additional profit of Rs 290,000 (US$ 5,472) after deducting transportation costs.

In order to solve the problem of transportation, the villagers have bought three jeeps, which run daily to the nearest town. This has not only improved and increased communication in general, it has also provided easy access to many facilities. The absence of health facilities was always a problem. Before the construction of the road, it used to take four to 10 people to carry a patient on a bed to the hospital. Besides this, every jeep brings in an income of Rs 328,500 (US$ 6,198) a year for their owners. The villagers also have plans to buy farm machinery, including tractors and threshers, now that they have a road.

DEVELOPING HUMAN CAPITAL AT VILLAGE LEVEL

The RSPs are the largest development training organisations in the country. Additionally, they also provide training in various aspects of rural development to the government, international agencies such as the World Bank and the United Nations, and other NGOs. The major focus of the RSPs however remains the training of male and female villagers, which can be divided under three separate sections:

- Managerial and leadership training enables villagers to assume management roles within community organisations: they manage CO meetings; ensure attendance; enhance savings and their utilisation; are adept at bookkeeping; facilitate long and short-term planning of the COs; and co-ordinate between the CO, RSPs, and other private and public agencies.
- Technical training enables villagers to become specialists: they then provide services to other villagers in matters ranging from crop improvement to livestock management and production, forestation, fisheries, improved agricultural technology and methods, health and education.
- There are around 70 subjects in which vocational training is currently offered, ranging from driving to carpet making to carpentry.

The impact of some of these community training projects is outlined below.

DEVELOPING EXPERTISE IN THE MANAGEMENT OF NATURAL RESOURCES

Noor Bibi is a vegetable, poultry and livestock specialist living in the northern areas of Pakistan. The following is an extract from an interview conducted with her.

Q. *What difference has the training made to your traditional vegetable growing practises?*
A. I feel it has made a big difference. Before the training, I used to cultivate vegetables on less land and there were always disease and pest attacks on the vegetables, and we did not know how to counter them. Now I use new seed varieties and new cultivation methods, and if there is a disease attack I can treat my vegetables. My family and I survive on vegetables; earlier we grew less, now much more. We used to eat dried vegetables and now we have fresh vegetables to eat.

Q. *Do you sell vegetables?*
A. The RSP has told us about vegetable marketing and with increased produce, I have been selling vegetables for the past three years. My yearly income from vegetable sales is Rs 8,000 (US$ 150).

Q. *What difference has this made to your everyday life?*
A. Earlier our household had no source of regular income. My husband had to work in the village as a labourer, but not on a regular basis. Whatever income I earned from vegetables or other crops (such as fruit or wheat), I spent on my children's education and household needs. We have educated our four sons and now wish that I had educated at least one of my daughters. Today life's problems are not the same, our household's situation is much improved. My husband and I have opened up a small shop in my village where I sell vegetables also.

Q. *As a woman, what difference has this made to your life?*
A. Earlier we had hardly any clothes or shoes to wear. We used to look at the other people and feel envious. Now, with my earnings, I can get whatever I want for myself. I feel proud at being able to earn myself. Unlike before, all members of our CO are now selling fruit and vegetables. Everyone wants to earn in order to have a better future.

Another example of the type of training that the RSPs provide in natural resource management is training in veterinary care. In rural areas, government veterinary service delivery is inadequate. Training in animal husbandry has helped villagers to reduce the instances of disease and death. It has also been instrumental in raising animal productivity, thereby increasing their market values. Because trained villagers provide services at people's doorsteps, poor people are able to afford treatment for their animals, and save on transportation costs and the higher charges levied by government veterinary services. At the same time, specialists are able to earn reasonable incomes. In order to increase awareness of the importance of proper animal husbandry, specialists conduct vaccination and de-worming campaigns. A survey undertaken in the district of Charsadda in the North-West Frontier Province showed that of the 106 men trained so far as livestock extension workers, around 67 per cent were active, while 33 per cent were less active or inactive. The RSPs provide training in all aspects of the management of natural resources and also specialist training in activities such as date processing, bee keeping and grain storage.

ENHANCING OFF-FARM SKILLS

To impart vocational training, the RSPs link villagers with government vocational training institutes or procure them apprenticeship placements with local craftsmen and artisans. The CO selects the trainees it wants to send on courses, and the villagers have to contribute towards part of their training, which ensures that only those villagers who have a genuine desire to use skills for income generation proceed on courses. When government institutes are used, the curriculum is modified so that the length and content of the course is more appropriate for the situation of the trainees. The vocational training most demanded by villagers is tailoring. This is because it is popular with both sexes, as opposed to other training which, due to prevailing social attitudes, only men can do, such as welding. Tailoring has been found to give immediate steady returns and is in great demand.

A study conducted in Kashmir in December 1998 to assess the impact of vocational training, showed that 75 per cent of the trainees had no work prior to the training, and 95 per cent of the women trainees did not work before the training. After the training, 62 per cent of the trainees were utilising their learned skills, earning an average net income of Rs 1,885 (US$ 36) per month. For female trainees, this average was Rs 622 (US$ 12) per month. It further showed that upon starting their own business, each trainee, on average, had employed and imparted further training to two additional people.

TRAINING IN MIDWIFERY AND CHILDCARE

A survey carried out of 122 village women who were trained as female health workers by the RSPs in the North-West Frontier Province showed that 48 per cent were highly active earning around Rs 750 (US$ 14) per month, 48 per cent were less active, earning Rs 350 (US$ 7) a month, while 15 per cent were not active at all. Similarly, in southern Baluchistan, the data on trained birth attendants (TBAs) trained by RSPs reveal that most of them are working efficiently and are being remunerated by the community. Survey results show that on average, a TBA's annual earnings range from Rs 17,000 to Rs 20,000 (US$ 320 to 377). According to the TBAs, they have brought infant/mother mortality rates down from 18–20 per cent to two or three per cent. In this area, as is the case throughout Baluchistan, the majority of villages lack basic health facilities, and women in particular suffer greatly as a result. During childbirth, the only available help comes from the local midwife. Ameena, for example, had been practising midwifery but was not aware of modern preventative and safety practices. The village women nominated her for a TBAs' course, which she attended

Table 1.2

Analysis of the vocational training portfolio

Vocation	Performance Indicators for the Trainees in each Discipline				
	Respondents utilising skills (Percentage)	Respondents not utilising skills (Percentage)	Average net income earned/ month (Rs)	Total no. of people employed by respondents	Total no. of people trained by respondents
Building/electricians	62	38	6,778	27	27
Tailoring	87	13	842	12	43
A/c or refrigeration	33	67	1,675	2	2
Auto-electrician	0	100	0	0	0
Welding	63	37	740	5	4
Plumbing and pipe fitting	50	50	2,700	1	4
TV/VCR repair	33	67	10,000	1	1
Auto mechanic	40	60	543	1	4
Computer	0	100	0	0	0
Total				49	85

Source: 'Human Resource Development', *NRSP Sixth Annual Report*, p. 38.

along with 15 other females from adjoining villages. After receiving training, she is apprising women in the area of health safety measures and basic health education. TBAs not only provide proper and timely services at the time of delivery, they also assist in linking women with local hospitals and population welfare departments, so that they can gain access to family planning services. In many cases, they also provide assistance in other health-related matters, such as providing iodised salt, immunisation and dietary advice.

PROVIDING CHILDREN WITH EDUCATION OPPORTUNITIES

The RSPs have directly set up a network of community-based schools throughout the country. The schools provide access to education for children, especially girls, using a modern teaching methodology that allows for the multi-dimensional growth of the child. Several features in the design of the school systems ensure that problems commonly faced by the public sector are averted:

- teacher absenteeism is avoided by recruiting a teacher from the village;
- daily school monitoring is carried out by a village education committee of five villagers who are trained by the RSPs to be able to manage the administrative aspects of the schools;
- in order to inspire a sense of ownership, the villagers are responsible for the space provision for the school;
- the parents have to pay a school fee that is decided by the CO, so that they understand that education has a value.

These schools have only one room, and this poses a challenge for teachers who have to address more than one class at a time. Appropriate training for teachers is arranged by the RSPs which train the teachers in multi-grade teaching methods. The cost of running the schools is either borne entirely by the villagers, or jointly by the villagers and a donor agency. A unique approach taken in the case of some schools has been the establishment of endowment funds of Rs 100,000–Rs 200,000 (US$ 1,887–US$ 3,774) each, through money provided by a donor. The interest earnings from these amounts are used to pay teacher salaries and other running expenses.

ENHANCING THE QUALITY OF HEALTH

The health programmes of the RSPs aim to create local capacity in the villages through the training of health workers and TBAs, raising awareness about health and hygiene issues and linking communities with existing service outlets. RSPs organise periodic health camps, where doctors, nurses, and other paramedical staff from government agencies or other NGOs are invited to deliver services to the villagers. The purpose of these camps is to motivate the village women to adopt family planning methods, and to establish a regular linkage between the villagers, the local women's health workers and the government's health services in the area. The RSPs also seek to foster formalised linkages, so in February 1999 the Population Welfare Ministry of the government of Pakistan issued a directive to all its departments in the country to co-operate with the RSPs.

FROM POVERTY TO PROSPERITY: THE ACHIEVEMENT
OF ONE VILLAGE

The Umari Kuhan village, in Pakistan's poorest and least developed province of Baluchistan, is comprised of 40 households which have lived here for generations. The village has two *karez* systems and the people's main source of earning is agriculture.

According to the villagers, prior to the formation of the community organisation, they hardly met as a group. They would get together to work on their *karez*, or on marriages or deaths, but otherwise months could pass without their meeting each other. Now they meet twice a month, and discuss issues and problems in their meetings. That is why now, as described in the following pages, they have overcome many of the problems they used to face.

Lack of Water: With the aid of the local RSP, the villagers have increased the volume of water in their *karez*, and started cultivating previously uncultivable land. A single *karez* normally consists of 14 *hangams* (approximately 8 acres of land) which need 12 hours of water. Fifty-two households are benefiting from this *karez*.

Low Productivity of Farms: After the extension of the *karez*, the members identified quality seed as their next need. Because they lacked this, their production was low. The RSP established a demonstration plot of Irri-6-type rice, which was very successful. This was shown to all the surrounding villages, too. The villagers of Umeri Kuhan were given the responsibility of supplying seed to other villagers, and now all villages in the area cultivate the same seed and sell the produce. The extension of the *karez* has enabled rice production to increase from 1,800 kg per *hangam* to 3,000 kg per *hangam*, amounting to Rs 16,800 (US$ 317). For all 14 *hangams* of Umeri Kuhan, this equates to Rs 235,200 (US$ 4,434).

Broad beans are also cultivated in large quantities and the extension of the *karez* has doubled their area of cultivation. Broad beans fetch a reasonably good price of Rs 35–40 (US$ 0.44–0.75) per kg, as they are harvested earlier here than in other areas.

Lack of Technology—The Husking Machine: After the rise in rice production, villagers came forward with the need for a husking machine. Until now, they had gone to the nearest town to have their rice husked and, on average, the cost was Rs 200 (US$ 3.77) per bag. The RSP provided a loan of Rs 135,000 (US$ 2,547) for a villager to install a husking machine, where the cost of husking a bag of rice is Rs 80 (US$ 1.5). Villagers thus save Rs 20 (US$ 0.38) per bag.

Pests on Crops: The Department of Agriculture is virtually non-existent in this area as it lacks provision of any medicines or seeds. Pests or disease have invariably destroyed the crops of villagers. One villager, Murad Ali, undertook agricultural training with the assistance of the RSP in the area. He now advises villagers regarding insecticides and pesticides, and has helped prevent the outbreak of diseases and pest attacks.

Death of Livestock: Goats in nearly every household would routinely succumb to disease. On average, two to three goats per household would die annually, and sometimes as many as eight to 10. Since a village member has been trained in veterinary care, however, the livestock mortality rate in the village has reduced drastically.

Lack of Insecticides and Pesticides: Previously, there was neither an agri-inputs supply store, nor did the Department of Agriculture have any provisions. This lack of pesticides and insecticides resulted in damage to crops. Villagers used to go to Karachi and Quetta to obtain necessary items. However, the RSP has since helped two villagers to open an agri-input store on the main road, through a loan of Rs 60,000 (US$ 1,132). They are fulfilling the needs of the entire area.

Lack of Communication and Electricity: The village sent a resolution to the government telecommunications department and has been approved to receive telephone connections. The villagers installed poles at their own expense for this. The village has also been assured the supply of electricity.

The CO manager, Mohammed Assa, credits all these development initiatives to CO formation. Umeri Kahun's development is typical of the progress that many RSP-fostered COs throughout Pakistan have made.

MEASURING IMPACT AND THE REDUCTION IN LEVELS OF POVERTY

The RSPs continue to monitor carefully, their work to assess the level at which poverty is diminishing. It has been 18 years since the oldest RSP, the AKRSP started operations. Data collected by the AKRSP through very large-scale Farm Household Income and Expenditure Surveys has shown that poverty reduced from 61 per cent to 33 per cent in the Baltistan region; from 42 per cent to 23 per cent in the Gilgit region; and from 43 per cent to 36 per cent in Chitral in the period 1991–97. In these regions, the AKRSP has covered almost the entire rural population. At the same time, per capita incomes in the northern area, as a proportion of national per capital incomes, increased from 27 per cent to 55 per cent in Baltistan; from 36 per cent to 68 per cent in Gilgit; and from 37 per cent to 52 per cent in Chitral.

Similarly, during the last year, the NRSP conducted a survey to assess the level to which it had enhanced villagers' incomes. Its results showed that since its inception, the NRSP has spent Rs 414 million (US$ 7.8 million) on operational expenses. In turn, it has increased the wealth of villagers by Rs 5.6 billion or US$ 107 million. These estimates were based on random surveys undertaken in different areas of Pakistan where the organisation operates. These calculations do not include social or indirect economic benefits, which the organisation says in many cases have had a much greater impact than the monetary returns. These calculations also exclude many activities whose quantification has not been attempted, such as literacy programmes, training programmes and social mobilisation activities. All the RSPs continue to use participatory monitoring techniques to evaluate the impact that their work is having on the target population.

WORKING WITH THE GOVERNMENT

In a country where succeeding governments have often suspended programmes initiated by the preceding government, and sometimes even sought to dismantle institutions created under previous programmes, changes of government have meant frequent disruptions in the development process. In this period of uncertainty, development practitioners have come to understand that development can only be realised when local communities form their own institutions, independent of government control.

Governments in Pakistan have been characterised by massive corruption and inefficiency. On the flip side of the coin, though, they also own most of the country's financial resources and its social infrastructure. In this context, the RSPs believe that rather than advocating and agitating against the government, and setting up parallel technical programmes, they should facilitate the increase in access of the rural poor to the services and inputs provided by the government, and should encourage government in planning and implementing activities with the active involvement of the rural poor. This is because people then 'own' and manage projects undertaken with their involvement. As explained above, when working with the RSPs, villagers are involved at every stage of the project from need identification and planning to implementation and maintenance, and have to contribute both financially and physically. Making the government understand this has taken the RSPs more than a decade. The fostering of linkages in Kashmir is typical of what the RSPs have had to experience at the national level. 'This philosophy will not work and can never be implemented', was the general comment of officials when the RSPs started working there. Additionally, as the RSPs gained acceptance amongst the communities, they were seen as a threat by the line departments, which thought they were bent upon making the latter redundant and minimising their role. In order to eradicate this misunderstanding, the RSPs have indulged heavily in public relations exercises with government officials and politicians, have invited them to workshops and seminars, and arranged visits to community organisations to demonstrate the effectiveness of the participatory approach. Since then, subsequent governments have been amongst the biggest advocates of the RSPs' work. In many districts of the country, heads of government departments concerned with agriculture, livestock, forestry, soil conservation, sanitation, rural works, health, and education, amongst others, meet and plan with the RSPs on a monthly basis at district planning meetings. Government officials are regular participants at conferences where office-bearers of COs gather and, in many cases, the former now directly approach COs.

The RSPs work in a politically unstable environment where public relations with the government of the day is of primary importance, especially as the RSPs intend to take their approach to scale. Similarly, the government has recognised that in order to reach out to the poor, as well as for cost efficiency and sustainability of village-based projects, it requires the active support of the RSPs.

The interesting aspect of these institutional linkages is their apolitical character. Despite the political instability of the country, the institutional collaboration at the grassroots level between the government, RSPs and community organisations, has always been consistent because of the non-political nature of the relationship. At the same time, the management of RSPs has been very successful in influencing government policies and structures through dialogue with the political leadership. Different political leaderships in the country have always been supportive of the philosophy and work of RSPs in the national development, and consequently have never attempted to politicise these institutions.

However, it has not been a simple and straightforward procedure. Capacity building for government workers has been a constraint to RSPs as their training departments possess limited resources for training the high number of government workers. Likewise, though the linkages between community organisations and government line agencies are worthwhile, there has also been a consistent hesitation on the part of the Government to institutionalise these linkages by making public sector departments accountable to the people. Additionally, the RSPs have also faced difficulties in such partnerships. In the seven large-scale area development projects where the RSPs work under contract with government, the RSPs have faced many difficulties, including slow release of payments owed to them and uncooperative attitudes of some government officials.

Similarly, lack of female staff in government line departments has also forced RSPs to recruit female technical staff to work with village women. The RSPs are continuing to hire and train more female staff in key programme areas, sectors and at all levels. Training of all staff (male and female) in gender issues and integrated planning is a part of this strategy.

In the newer partnerships with the government, more systematic approaches to linkage-building have been introduced. The government line agencies are involved in a step-by-step approach to clarifying their terms of partnership and deciding what input they need to give at each stage of the planning and implementation process. The role of each line agency is agreed and formalised in the form of standard operating procedures for integrated village-based planning and implementation. Where RSPs once used to approach government line agencies as needed, increasingly all co-operating agencies are undertaking joint field visits for key steps in the project cycle, according to a common monthly work plan. Government line agencies are even involved in diagnostic surveys[8]. On the one hand, this makes public officers accountable to the people, while on the other it helps to change the mind-set of government functionaries.

In October, 2002, Pakistan witnessed parliamentary elections, which ushered in a new civilian government after 3 years of military rule. During the 3-year stint of General Pervez Musharraf as Chief Executive of the country, the RSPs had developed a good working relationship with the government at both the federal and provincial levels. The military government had encouraged the growth of RSPs and its key members were active supporters of the model. The elections of 2002 were preceded by the formation of district governments throughout the country and greater decentralisation of power to the grassroots. It is at this—the field level, that the RSPs have had extraordinary success. Many villagers associated with RSPs have won seats, RSPs have succeeded in securing the good will of district and Union Council councillors and are active in collaborating with district governments to more efficiently implement development projects.

SUSTAINABILITY OF THE WORK OF THE RSPS

The sustainability of village and community organisations is an issue that is often debated within RSPs. The strategy of the RSPs is to strengthen and develop the capacities of COs to manage and implement their development initiatives independently; and evolve partnerships and collaborations with public sector departments, donors and private organisations. Members of community organisations are mobilised and supported in seeking independent funding from donors. At the same time, savings are promoted as a local pool of capital to ensure financial sustainability of grass-roots institutions. Records of savings made by the CO, expenditure on physical infrastructure, schools and other projects undertaken, and credit borrowed from the RSP are maintained by the villagers. This record maintenance promotes transparency and equity of benefits for greater accountability at the village level. RSPs believe that the development of communities is neither a linear nor a time-bound process, and hence does not imply a narrow definition of assessing institutional maturity. At the same time, there is a constant effort to develop activists to take over development activities, and the number of such activists is growing. An example is Khatima Bibi, a widow in the district of Kohat in the North-West Frontier Province. She was trained as a birth attendant by the RSP, and now deals with child delivery cases. Having received training in various subjects, she imparts training to village women in vegetable growing, shampoo, candle and soap making. She is instrumental in encouraging growth in savings in her CO and has assisted the RSP in the formation of a number of other female COs. Currently, she is receiving training in forestry.

Furthermore, the RSPs' long-term commitment to develop and empower the 38 million people of Pakistan living below the poverty line cannot be served without ensuring the sustainability of the RSPs themselves. The AKRSP, the oldest RSP, can claim to have included 85 per cent of the population in its programme area. However other RSPs have much lower coverage. The approach cannot be replicated throughout the country without securing more funds. At present the RSPs depend heavily on the government, and bilateral and multilateral funding. For making their operations sustainable, some of the RSPs have considered building endowment funds. Some of them have been provided with seed capital by the Pakistan government to sustain their work. However, bearing in mind the volatility of Pakistan's political situation, RSPs have to seek other options to reduce their reliance on the government and donors. They can do this in two main ways. First, the training departments in the RSPs can become an income-generating source, and second, RSPs could charge fees from their donors over and above the cost of any project or programme. This fee could be interpreted as a service charge paid by the donors to an RSP for providing institutional support to the communities as an intermediary organisation.

The other form of sustainability that needs to be ensured is that of linkages. Will community organisations be able to exert pressure on the line agencies to 'deliver' in the absence of intermediary support organisations? The onus for ensuring this lies with the government. If, as seems to be the case, the government feels that the RSPs have the most suited approach to alleviate poverty in Pakistan, then institutional reforms need to be brought about in the country.

Ever since I completed my education six years ago, I have worked for the RSPs. I continue to work for them because I believe that the approach they advocate is the best one. It is quick, simple and effective—entrusting people with the responsibility to undertake their own development. One of the most motivating comments I heard was a few years ago when, on a trip to Dera Ismail Khan, an old villager told us, 'Since I was born, no one has come to ask what state we live in. You are the first people who have come to ask about our conditions'. Since then, I have often heard this comment. In these trying times, the RSPs may be the only ray of hope for the rural poor of Pakistan.

NOTES AND REFERENCES

1. Cover story, *Liberal Times*, January 1998, pp. 31–34.
2. This includes all five districts of the northern areas and three of the seven districts of Azad Jammu and Kashmir.
3. The Baluchistan Rural Support Programme (BRSP) has recently commenced operations. Details of its achievements are thus excluded from this report.
4. *The Asian*, 5 July 1999.
5. *Annual Review*, AKRSP, 1998.
6. **Hussein. M, H. W. Khan, Z. Alam** and **T. Hussain**, 'An Interim Evaluation of Irrigation Projects Undertaken by AKRSP in Gilgit District of Northern

Pakistan' (AKRSP, 1986) and *WB Evaluation Reports of AKRSP* (1987, p. 42; 1995, p. 22).

7. *The News*, 2 December, 1998.

8. Diagnostic survey is a tool employed by RSPs in identifying village-level priorities and establishing project design parameters. This approach places confidence in the villagers' ability to identify their priorities and, through the process of interactive dialogues, determines both the feasibility of the project and the responsibilities of each party in project implementation.

2

The Women's Centre for Change, Penang: Empowering the Women of Malaysia

Siti Hawa Ali

A PERSONAL ENCOUNTER

Coming back from school that day, I saw my uncle talking to my mother very intensely. He did not even notice me. This was my eldest uncle. He was known to all of us—his nieces and nephews—as a comedian, but that day he wasn't even smiling. I was very curious but dared not sit near them. We were not allowed to listen in on adults' conversations—it was considered rude. I tried to walk past them several times, but my mother finally gave me a sharp look, which I knew was a signal not to eavesdrop. But I had already overheard that someone had been beaten quite badly and hospitalised. I learnt from my mother later that my eldest cousin (my uncle's eldest daughter) had been beaten up by her husband. My uncle was apparently devastated and seemed at a loss because she was his favourite daughter. My sisters and I were reminded not to tell anyone. I asked my mother how the matter would be resolved—she did not know. According to my mother, when my cousin was well enough, she would go back to her husband. At that time I remembered wondering how ridiculous it was to expect a person to go back to someone who had hurt her. To me, the solution was quite simple: I asked my mother as to why the rest of the family couldn't hit the man in return, especially since this was how I would have dealt with big bullies in my school. My friend and I would never allow the boys to bully us. Instead we would get into a 'battle' and fight them to the end. But as my mother said, it was not that simple.

In retrospect, I think many of my relatives could not believe that my cousin had been abused. She had always appeared very happy whenever she came to visit us with her husband and I remember thinking that she must have been happy since she had everything—a house, a car, a salaried husband. I came to know much later that my cousin and her six

I wish to thank the volunteers and staff of the Women's Centre for Change for their support and co-operation in the research for this paper.

children were regularly abused, both physically and emotionally, and that she had to work to supplement the family income. The tall, well-built handsome lady ended up looking so old and tired. She died in an accident at her workplace, thus bringing her suffering to an end. She had been married to her husband for 16 years and only God knows how long and how often she had been abused.

I did not hear any more stories of domestic abuse after that, maybe because I was still too young and too busy with myself. But I began to think about the issue seriously after I read a book by Erin Pizzey called *Scream Quietly or Your Neighbour Will Hear* in early 1983, eight years after my cousin passed away. In 1984 I joined the Women's Crisis Centre (now known as Women Centre for Change and henceforth WCC). Since then, I have not stopped hearing stories of women and children being abused.

INTRODUCTION

I am going to share with you the story and experience of WCC[1], a small women's organisation in the state of Penang, in the northern region of peninsular Malaysia. The organisation focuses on the struggle of liberating women and female children from all types of violence. I will begin by giving a brief summary of my country, Malaysia, followed by a discussion of the context and issues that shaped the WCC. Subsequently, I will describe the development of the WCC and try to highlight its organisational structure, its mode of operation and the linkages the WCC has with other organisations, as well as with the government. The objective is to show how a small voluntary organisation has succeeded in empowering women, as also the difficulties and problems embedded in this process.

The facts of my story are drawn largely from my experience as a volunteer, a member of the management group and an activist of the organisation. I have worked with the organisation since its inception in 1985. For the purpose of this paper, I will also draw on the experience and perceptions of some of my colleagues as well as other volunteers and activists of the WCC. All this has been cross-checked with official records from the WCC, so that memories reflect true facts and the account is comprehensive. However, the arguments and the conclusions made are my own and do not represent either my colleagues or the WCC.

THE CONTEXT: MALAYSIA

Malaysia consists of peninsular Malaysia, which is made up of 12 states, and the states of Sabah and Sarawak in Borneo. These are organised in a federal system, with Kuala Lumpur as the administrative capital. It has 330,000 sq km of land area with a total population of 23.27 million (in 2000). The total GDP (1998) was RM 131.25 billion, with an annual growth rate of more than 8 per cent in the 1980s and the 1990s until the economic crisis of 1997. The per capita income in 2000 was RM 13,359, representing a drastic change from RM 1,071 in 1970 when development efforts were stepped up. To introduce the country in greater detail, it is necessary to describe briefly the people, the economy, politics and government, and in the context of this paper, the position of women in Malaysia.

People

Malaysia is a multi-ethnic country. Historically, it emerged out of British colonial labour policy, which imported Chinese and Indian labourers to work in tin mines and rubber plantations in pre-independence Malaya. Through naturalisation and granting of citizenship at the time of independence, the Malaysian population today consists of the *Bumiputra* (the indigenous population), the Chinese, Indians and others. In 2000, the *Bumiputra* constituted the majority (66.1 per cent), followed by the Chinese (25.3 per cent), the Indians (7.4 per cent) and others (1.23 per cent). There were also a substantial number of non-citizens who made up 1.23 million of the total population.

In terms of geographical distribution, the *Bumiputra* population is divided into the Malays, who are Muslims, in peninsular Malaysia, and other indigenous populations (such as Kadazan, Dusun, Dayak and Iban) in Sabah and Sarawak, who are largely non-Muslims (Christians and other local religions). The Chinese are quite well distributed in the peninsula, Sabah and Sarawak, representing 25–30 per cent of the local population. They are mainly Buddhists, with a small Christian minority. The Indians are mostly located in the peninsula and are largely Hindu.

Although Islam is the national religion and Malay culture is sanctioned as the basis of national culture, thus placing the Malays in a dominant position, other ethnic groups are free to practise and promote their respective cultures and religions. This has resulted in the development of distinct cultures and identities among the ethnic groups in the country. While they are easily distinguishable into Malays, Chinese, Indians, Kadazans and Ibans, their religious, cultural, and social sensitivities differentiate them into distinct localities, economic activities, areas of social interaction, associations and political struggles.

However, due to decades of nation-building through a common language (Bahasa Malaysia), a single national education system and some degree of residential and employment mix, the ethnic groups relate to one another with a fair amount of tolerance and understanding. Though there is some inter-ethnic association (such as belonging to the same workplace, clubs and societies, and inter-marriage), Malaysians of different ethnic groups largely relate to one another in a functional way. In fact, ethnic antagonisms are seldom expressed openly because the government takes a harsh stand on ethnic sensitivities and suppresses ethnic antagonism upon the slightest symptom.

Economy

In terms of economic status, however, the different ethnic groups do not share the economy equally. For instance, the *Bumiputra* were lagging behind other ethnic groups in terms of wealth ownership. In 1970, *Bumiputra* individuals and trust agencies in peninsular Malaysia owned a meagre 2.4 per cent of share capital in the country compared to the Chinese (27.2 per cent), Indians (1.1 per cent) and foreigners (36.6 per cent). At the same time, the incidence of rural poverty reached 58.7 per cent, with the smallholders totalling 64.4 per cent, fishermen 73.2 per cent and paddy planters 88.1 per cent. This affected the Malays in particular since most of them lived in rural areas.

To avoid political and social instability caused by Malay poverty, the government launched its New Economic Policy (NEP) in 1971. The objective was to integrate the *Bumiputra* community into mainstream economic development, with the target of achieving 30 per cent *Bumiputra* equity in the total wealth of the country. Poverty was to be eradicated and society restructured so that employment and income differences would not be identified with ethnicity. The government controlled the economy on behalf of the *Bumiputra*, but without affecting the development of the market. Indeed, the government accelerated market development by creating government enterprises and competing in the market on behalf of the *Bumiputra* community. This NEP strategy became the core of Malaysian five-year development plans in subsequent years and was reflected in the *Bumiputra* quota for business opportunities, education and training, employment, house ownership and ownership of share capital.

The launch of the NEP coincided with the process of industrialisation which, in turn, depended largely on the internationalisation of production by multinational companies into Malaysia. Free industrial zones were set up and favourable concession packages were offered to multinationals in order to encourage foreign investment. This proved quite successful, and by the 1980s, the structure of the economy had changed from one based on agriculture to one based on manufacturing and services. The economy began to rely more on manufactured exports than raw materials, as it had in the 1960s. This was followed by a rapid rural–urban migration which created new urban centres, as well as expanded the existing ones. Subsequently, the pattern of employment changed, with the rise of an industrial working class as well as a new middle class.

In general, the Malaysian economy was sufficiently prepared for greater liberalisation by the time Malaysia was absorbed into globalisation processes in the early 1990s. Carrying on the spirit of the NEP, a New Development Plan (NDP) was launched for the period 1990–2000 to offer the private sector greater participation and more foreign direct investment. This propelled Malaysia into the high growth era of the early 1990s. Manufactured exports continued to be the backbone of the economy, and labour force participation in the manufacturing sector grew, marking the change of the economy into a modern industrial phase. The current growth of new industries, such as information technology, added new impetus to the growing economy.

Three decades of rapid growth since the 1970s brought about general affluence and a new consumerist lifestyle for Malaysians. At the same time, their quality of life also improved significantly; there was a significant increase in the rate of literacy, school enrolment, health facilities, life span and the position of women. Official documents claim that the quality of life in Malaysia is comparable, if not similar, to that in developed countries. Together with almost full employment (unemployment was below 3.9 per cent in 1998), a high per capita income, reasonable distribution of income and a declining rate of poverty (6.1 per cent in 1997), economic development and affluence have created social and political stability.

Politics and Government

The government has played a major role in the development of the Malaysian economy and society. It is generally agreed that aggressive policies such as the NEP and the NDP were instrumental in changing Malaysia into what it is today. But because the policies were highly discriminatory in favour of the *Bumiputra* population, especially the Malays, the government defended itself through means which, in many instances, appeared harsh and authoritarian. Following the introduction of the NEP, for instance, the government implemented a set of new laws, such as the 1971 Sedition Act, prohibiting the questioning of special privileges given to *Bumiputra*. Likewise, to curb the voices of critical NGOs, the government enacted the Societies Act in 1987. All this complemented the infamous Internal Security Act (ISA) which makes government opponents and critics liable for detention without trial. It is understandable that these laws were necessary to bring the *Bumiputra* community into mainstream development, for persistent Malay poverty would be politically explosive. But as a result, the development of a civil society has been somewhat hampered. For instance, citizens are not free to express their opinions on matters deemed sensitive (such as ethnic issues), union activities are largely curbed, the media is controlled and censored, and there is a law prohibiting a gathering of more than three people without a police permit.

Nevertheless, some form of democracy exists in Malaysia. Citizens are free to form associations, including political parties, and choose their government. The general elections of 1999 showed that political democracy was indeed alive and well. Even the ruling parties in the government failed to hold back the onslaught of opposition parties. But since the people are highly divided along ethnic lines, political parties are no more than representations of particular ethnic groups. For instance, in Peninsular Malaysia the United Malays National Organisation (UMNO) largely represents the interests of secular Malays, the Malayan Chinese Association (MCA) represents the middle-class Chinese, and the Malayan Indian Congress (MIC) represents the Indians. Likewise, political parties in Sabah and Sarawak follow similar ethnic divides; for instance, the Kadazan support the Parti Bersatu Sabah and Dayak the Parti Bansa Dayak Sarawak. In order to gain power and form a government, political parties that share similar goals usually form an inter-ethnic coalition known as the National Front and negotiate the terms among themselves.

Though the dominant partner in the coalition, the UMNO, may dictate terms to the other ethnic groups, the decision of the government reflects the interests of the coalition and its members. This is transmitted down to their supporters, making them amenable to government policies. Those who criticise the government and the coalition policies form their own political parties and constitute the Opposition. Although more popular than in the past, the Opposition has been rather weak. This gives the government an almost absolute power to devise policies and strategies to develop the country and the people as it deems fit. The people, however, demand greater freedom, transparency and accountability in the system of governance and a more civil society.

Position of Women in Society

Women constitute about half the population of Malaysia, about 11.4 million (2000), but they make up about 44.3 per cent of the 9.6 million labour force (2000). This means that a large proportion of them are either dependents or remain in informal and the unpaid labour sector. However, the transformation of Malaysia into an industrial economy brought about significant changes to the position of women in society. To begin with, there has been an increase in the number of women obtaining formal education. In 1993, for instance, about 50 per cent of women in the labour force had secondary education, and 11 per cent of them had tertiary education. Traditionally, women's education had been confined mostly to the arts and humanities, but by 1994 women constituted 40.4 per cent of the enrolment in vocational courses. The general trend is that more and more women are being absorbed into mainstream employment, including those in professional and managerial positions. The rate of labour force participation among women also increased from 37.2 per cent in 1970 to 44.5 per cent in 2000. This is the result of a general government policy of equal opportunities in education and employment. In addition, the government also protects women through various legislations guaranteeing their dignity, rights in marriage, and inheritance[2].

The rise in women's participation in the labour force saw a greater number of women being drawn into the urban industrial workforce. Following a general trend of rural–urban migration, a large proportion of these women belong to the rural indigent population that migrated to towns in search of employment. Being poorly educated and lacking specific skills, they are inevitably absorbed into low-wage, labour-intensive industrial jobs, mainly in production and related work. In 2000, for instance, 27.3 per cent of women were employed as production and related workers in manufacturing industries. They also constituted 43.4 per cent of all labour in the manufacturing industry[3]. Being women, however, they get paid less than male workers, particularly in labour-intensive industries[4].

Nevertheless, the change in women's employment from rural to urban production work led to several important social changes. Women were now divided between their traditional roles as homemakers and the strict regime of the industrial workplace. Also, the spread of urbanisation tended to create nuclear families, denying women the traditional support system from members of the extended family. As a general policy, the government does encourage employers to provide support systems for women, such as crèches at work, flexible working hours, and part-time work, so that more women could be absorbed into the work force. This became necessary when Malaysia began to suffer from a shortage of labour in the mid-1980s. In practice, however, urban and industrial work practices are strictly regimented, and require shift work and overtime, including weekends. Employers are mainly concerned about profits and rarely provide support to female workers. This has created a significant strain on women's domestic work, childcare and other traditional familial and social obligations. Given the lack of change in patriarchal expectations and the position of men in society, in general industrialisation and urbanisation have thrust even greater responsibilities on women. Inability to cope with the new burdens has led to a host of social complications, such as family breakdowns, juvenile delinquency, sexual violence and teenage pregnancies. In many cases, women—including young women—bear the main brunt of the problems. They are harassed, exploited, punished and violated in many ways both at home and at work.

WOMEN'S ORGANISATIONS IN MALAYSIA

The incidence of violence against women has always been rampant in Malaysian society. To a large extent, the issue was, and still is, considered a 'family matter' that must be kept private. If at all, the women who suffered received assistance only from informal sources such as family members and friends. Those who were 'brave enough' reported the problem to religious authorities or government agencies such as the police and the welfare department. On the whole, the issue was well hidden from the public, thus perpetuating the general perception that domestic violence was a 'family and private matter', where rape could only happen to 'loose women' who 'asked for it', and sexual harassment signified nothing but a 'cry for attention'. These perceptions clearly indicate male domination over women and a lack of insight on the subject matter. By the early 1980s, however, the scenario began to change. International concerns over the issue of discrimination and violence against women began to reach Malaysia. We can observe changes in the thinking about the problem at two levels: through the activities of the United Nations (UN) and its agencies, and secondly through the rise of women's organisations.

United Nations and Government Policies on Women

The Malaysian government has extended support to almost all women's programmes introduced by the UN. For instance, the 1975 Declaration of the United Nations Decade for Women to eliminate gender discrimination was adopted and the Malaysian government responded by setting up the National Advisory Council for the Integration of Women in Development (NACIWID) in 1976. The main task of the Council was to advise the government on women's participation in development. This was followed by the formation of the Women Secretariat (HAWA) in 1983 by the Prime Minister's department, with the sole purpose of ensuring that women participate in national development and that mechanisms are created for the purpose[5]. As a result, the National Women Policy was formulated and approved by the Cabinet in 1989 following the UN Third World Conference on Women in Nairobi in 1985. At the same time, changes were made to the rape law in 1989, culminating in the introduction of the Domestic Violence Act in 1994. By 1991, a special space had been created for women's development in the country's economic Five-Year Plans[6]. The government's concern for women's welfare was further augmented in 1995 when it approved the UN Convention to Eliminate all forms of Discrimination Against Women. In the strong belief that elimination of sexual harassment would increase productivity at work, the government later introduced the 'Code of Practice on the Prevention and Eradication of Sexual Harassment in the Workplace' in August 1999. Till date, however, only 10 companies have adopted the code in their daily work environment[7]. To ensure effective co-ordination and focus on women issues, the government set up the Ministry of Women Affairs in 2001.

To some extent, UN programmes not only reminded the government of women's issues both at the Malaysian and the international level, but also encouraged the latter to apply the programmes at the local level. Also, such a hold on the government made it slightly easier for women's groups to lobby and pressure for changes in policies for women. This was what the women's groups in Kuala Lumpur did— besides having the advantage of a large concentration of concerned women in the capital, they had better access to government department headquarters located in Kuala Lumpur. Groups located away from Kuala Lumpur, such as those in Penang, were either consulted for discussion and planning or were asked to endorse proposals and resolutions reached by those in Kuala Lumpur. A brief history of their work has been documented in the following pages.

Rise of Women's Organisations

The history of women's organisations in Malaysia began in 1952 when the Women's Institute was established. Subsequently many other women's organisations were established following the creation of an umbrella body known as the National Council of Women's Organisations (NCWO) in 1960[8]. The NCWO plays an advisory and consultative role to its affiliates and the government, and was mainly involved in facilitating the women's agenda in national development. During this period, however, the NCWO and its affiliates did not focus on the problem of violence against women. For this reason, a group of concerned women in Petaling Jaya near Kuala Lumpur set up a separate organisation called the Women's Aid Organisation (WAO) in 1982. It focused specifically on the issue of violence against women, and received an immediate response from women who needed its services[9]. Since then, the issue began to emerge slowly but steadily. By March 1985, it began to snowball, when a group of women's organisations set up a joint action group with a workshop-cum-exhibition on violence against women in Kuala Lumpur[10].

Apart from the WAO, the 1980s also saw the emergence of many other women's organisations which assisted and provided shelter to victims of violence. These include the All Women's Action Society, which also focused on violence against women, and a number of other women's organisations in Kuala Lumpur. They constituted a group of NGOs which tackled issues relating to women workers, women's health, women and development, women and religion and legal advocacy work[11]. To a large extent, the growth of women's organisations was also strongly supported by the government. As noted above, it created a favourable environment for women to state their case, right into the 1990s.

DEVELOPMENT OF THE WOMEN'S CENTRE FOR CHANGE (WCC)

The Women's Centre for Change (WCC) could not have asked for a better environment in which to establish itself. The concern over violence against women and the model of organisation provided by women's groups in Kuala Lumpur became the driving force behind the establishment of the WCC. A group of women from diverse backgrounds, ethnic groups and fields of expertise came together to formulate the idea. They agreed that such an organisation was needed in northern Malaysia and that Penang was definitely the best location for it. Like Kuala Lumpur, Penang has a commendable historical background of voluntarism and civic consciousness. It also has sufficient resources in the form of professional support and an active business community. The registration process began in 1984, and by July 1985 the organisation was officially registered [12]. In May 2001, the official name of the organisation was changed to 'Women's Centre for Change'.

Goals and Objectives

The goal of the organisation is to promote a violence-free society through equal and respectful gender relationships for all Malaysians, irrespective of race or religion. It endeavours to create an environment conducive to achieving this objective. To begin with, the organisation focuses on women who are the victims and survivors of violence and provides them with immediate support services. Free assistance, in terms of emotional support, legal advice and temporary shelter are also given. The Centre also gives high priority to public education and consciousness-building through outreach programmes. In particular, the Centre intends to change the attitude of the authorities and to sensitise them to women's issues while targeting the local community in order to convince them that women's issues are worthy of attention. Legal advocacy and research are also considered critical in creating an environment conducive to women learning to develop themselves.

The WCC's Identity

The WCC was lucky in having volunteers who supported them, female and male, and who were very resourceful and committed to change. From its inception, the founders of the WCC made it clear that the organisation would not take a sexist position. While it was a women's organisation which championed women's rights and focused on addressing the problem of violence against women in an objective manner, it was also an open organisation and would acknowledge any contribution from women or men to tackle the issue.

As a NGO, however, WCC members were initially concerned about the 'charity' image that seems to haunt most service organisations. Since the service component is the core activity of the organisation, members were determined to free the organisation from the image. From the beginning, the Centre was determined to identify itself as an organisation which provided, among other things, services to abused women, and for this reason, and from the outset, the Centre has not provided financial or material relief to women who were not staying at the shelter. Should the need arise, the WCC would refer such women to other relevant organisations. In order to create an independent frame of mind among users, those who use the shelter services are also informed that they can only stay temporarily.

Similarly, members were concerned that the Centre remained singularly focused on women's issues. Since the problem transcends ethnicity, culture and religion, it was pertinent that the WCC maintains a multi-ethic and multi-religious identity. This is especially crucial as ethnicity and religion are extremely sensitive issues in Malaysian society. While unintentional 'abuse' of religion can offend an average person, communities as a whole may be easily aroused into open and direct action to protect their culture and beliefs.

Infrastructure

As distressed women immediately responded to the Centre, the WCC knew that its services were needed. At the beginning, it did not even have the proper premises to operate from, but service users were willing to meet WCC volunteers at any convenient location. The overwhelming reaction showed how badly a support group was needed and how critical the problem was in Penang.

The WCC's modest beginnings did not hamper the spirit of its volunteers. A year after registration, the Centre was able to provide telephonic and individual counselling from a small office rented from the local municipality. Volunteers were asked to manage the telephone counselling because at that stage very few women turned up for face-to-face assistance. It was possible that they were not certain of the organisation, but it was also probable that they were concerned over the stigma they would face if they were seen to be seeking help. At the time, the Centre did not have its own temporary shelter, but whenever the need arose, it sought assistance from other organisations. Efforts to obtain a building from the state government for an office as well as a shelter were not fruitful. This was definitely because women's issues were not given priority by the state authorities. It was only four years later, in 1989, when the committee members boldly availed of a bank loan, that the Centre managed to find a small house to be used as a permanent shelter. By 1990, the centre had received a long-term funding commitment from an international organisation[13]. This improved the position of the Centre in all respects; the volunteers could now concentrate on providing services without having to worry about financial matters. With careful financial administration, the Centre managed to buy another building which is currently used as the administrative office. The changes in the physical set-up of the organisation not only created more space for work and storage but also, most importantly, boosted the confidence of the volunteers and the image of the organisation as a whole.

Linkages with Other Women's Groups

The WCC maintains close ties with other women's organisations in order to be well-informed on the progress of women's issues and to develop a strong network of women's organisations in the country. The

Centre has also taken part in international women's programmes, such as those organised by the Network of Women Living Under Muslim Law based in Paris. The programme provided a forum for discussion at the international level and allowed WCC members to understand the situation of women in other countries at first hand. Participation in women's-group exchange programmes was another example of international linkages. This was done either at the regional or the international level and provided a forum for an exchange of ideas with international groups. Indirectly, this helped to sustain the interest of WCC members on the issues confronting them, while at the same time it developed their confidence and capacity to carry on.

STRUCTURE OF GOVERNANCE

According to Rajesh Tandon, 'The governance of NGOs focuses on the issues of policy and identity, rather than the issues of day-to-day implementation of programmes.' This implies that the primary issue of governance is to address the ' . . . issues of a NGO's vision, mission and strategy,' and to define 'norms and values that are the basis of institutional functioning'[14]. Having defined the overall philosophy of the organisation, it is then translated into action through the styles of management. In the case of the WCC, the guiding values of the organisation may be defined as promoting:

• women's rights (justice and dignity for women)
• multi-faith and multiculturalism (respect and acceptance of differences)
• power sharing (full participation)
• growth of an individual (building a person's potential and capacity in body, mind and spirit).

These values are clearly defined in the WCC's constitution, but somehow, throughout its 15-year-old history, the WCC has never come up with any vision or clear mission statements to the effect. It assumes that its members, especially the active volunteers, understand the mission of the organisation. Perhaps it is true that the members *do* understand the values of the organisation, but it is difficult to determine the extent to which they have adopted these values. This is especially true when the organisation is not free from the internal conflicts described as follows.

Management Structure

To bring its values into action, the WCC is managed by a team of volunteers organised into the General Committee. This consists of an elected Executive Committee (President, two Vice-Presidents, Secretary, Assistant Secretary and Treasurer) and the committee members. The General Committee also creates sub-committees from the membership base for particular activities, and members from the General Committee are given the responsibility to head the sub-committees.

For daily operations and management of the organisation, the General Committee is assisted by a team of salaried staff headed by an Executive Director. In terms of decision-making pertaining to organisational policies and programmes, this is usually done on a collective basis, either by a small group or by the General Committee. In urgent cases, the Executive Committee is given the authority to make speedy decisions. The final decision, however, rests with the members during annual general meetings. Any conflict or major changes in the policies of the organisation must be decided by the members in an extraordinary general body meeting, or the annual general body meetings, as stated by the constitution.

One observable outcome of this style of management is the development of a collective leadership. Every person in the committee knows that she is not entitled to any more power than the rest of the committee members. The positions in the General Committee may also change annually, but programmes and activities are usually conducted by sub-committees which run for a longer period. However, and with the exception of those delegated to the Executive Committee, sub-committees and the Executive Director, every decision has to be approved by the General Committee. This perhaps creates the balance of power in the running of the organisation.

Managing Power

Managing power has been the concern of the General Committee of the WCC since its inception. Many of us have observed power struggles in NGOs, either through personal experiences or research. Similar to other NGOs, we notice that there is a tendency among founder members or committee members to stay too long in the positions and 'own' the organisation. On the other hand, it is quite difficult to initiate changes in leadership because it may result in conflicts and power struggles, causing grave harm to the organisation.

In order to overcome such a situation and to ensure equal power sharing in the WCC, the organisation came up with a plan to rotate its General Committee periodically, which is stated clearly in the constitution. Except for the post of the President which is rotated annually, a person who is elected into a position in the Executive Committee may hold the office for only three years, but may remain in the General Committee for a total of five years, after which she has to step down for at least a year before she can be re-elected. This has been the practice for the last 15 years. One of the definite advantages of this practice is the creation of built-in checks and balances in the management of power. While this provides an opportunity for an active person to 'rest' from the organisation for a while, the system also discourages identification of the organisation with any particular individual—a phenomenon which can easily occur in the case of long-term leadership. At the same time, the system allows for a new person to move into the General Committee gradually.

The idea of individual capacity-building is also part of a power-sharing strategy. For instance, General Committee members were encouraged to take turns in chairing and recording discussion sessions. This system, however, worked only for a while because members are only willing to take turns in chairing meetings but not to take the role of a rapporteur. As a result, the normal practice of a president chairing meetings and a secretary taking notes, continues.

Like any manmade system, leadership monitoring too has its share of drawbacks. Since the election is held annually and the position of the President is continuously changed, there can be breaks in the continuity of ideas and activities. This is particularly burdensome for supporting staff because they have to deal with different personalities all the time. To some extent, this may also reduce the commitment of individuals (in the General Committee) because they know that they are in the position only for a short period of time. Similar to the case in note-taking during meetings, members are careful not to take on any extra burdens.

However, the management of the WCC has not suffered too badly from this problem so far. The Centre has a core group of leaders and volunteers who understand clearly the position and needs of the organisation. They provide continuity by incorporating younger members into a pool from which new leaders are selected. Gradually, they prepare for changes in the management leadership and sustain the struggle for women's causes.

Managing Staff

Currently the WCC has four full-time staff, including the Executive Director. All of them have a tertiary-level education and are qualified to carry out their duties. A qualified part-time volunteer, who is partly remunerated, also assists them. The WCC also takes pride in paying its staff well. One major mistake made by many voluntary organisations is that they tend to pay their staff charity salaries. The WCC realised that this not only shows disrespect, but also fails to sustain the interest of the staff concerned.

Generally, the members of the staff are given their duties according to their abilities and educational backgrounds. In most cases, this involves implementing the policies and programmes identified by the General Committee. The current relationship between the staff and committee members is quite open, with the former taking part in General Committee meetings. This contrasts with previous practice, when there was a hierarchy between the staff and committee members. At the time, the WCC was advised to change the arrangement and to allow staff to participate more actively in the organisational decision-making processes. Indeed, this change was necessary to ensure that the staff cultivated a sense of belonging to the organisation and did not simply behave as paid workers.

Financial Management

At the beginning of its development, the WCC relied mainly on local donations. Fund raising became a critical issue as donations received were not sufficient for the organisation to develop effective services and to run good programmes, and a great deal of volunteers' energy was directed towards this activity. But when the WCC received long-term funding from an overseas organisation, the financial situation immediately improved. This funding proved beneficial to the organisation, as the WCC could then concentrate more on its core activities. Nevertheless, the WCC continues to raise funds from local sources. Apart from generating income, the fund raising also generates interest and commitment among local people to support organisations such as the WCC. The organisation also received some financial assistance from the government, but the amount is almost insignificant: less than two per cent of the WCC's total annual expenditure.

It must be noted, however, that when the WCC was looking for possible donors and financial assistance, it made certain policy guidelines clear. First, donors do not erode the autonomy of the organisation. This is particularly critical because autonomy constitutes the heart of the organisation which uses empowerment as its major strategy. For this reason, it must not be tied up with conditions attached by any sponsor. Second, since October 1997, the WCC also decided not to approach the following sources for donations:

- any individual, groups or organisations involved in activities or actions that lower the dignity of women
- tobacco companies
- companies involved in the production of alcohol
- gambling organisations or companies
- organisations or countries that openly condone the oppression of women.

The primary reason for avoiding such sources is due to the fact that many women's problems arise from their spouses misusing the products produced by these companies, or from these organisations' promoting and condoning the source of women's and family misery. To avoid associating with them is to protest against their activities.

On the whole, the WCC has managed its funds well and managed to secure ownership of both the shelter and its administrative office. However, by the year 2001, the Centre will no longer receive long-term sponsorship from the current donor. To cope with an expected increase in future demand for the services, therefore, the organisation may have to seek new funding sources or devise mechanisms that will make it financially independent[15].

APPROACHES, ACTIVITIES AND SERVICES AT THE WCC

Approaches

From its inception, the WCC adopted two approaches to handle the problem of violence against women. One is the services-oriented approach, while the other is the gender-equity approach. The former focuses on helping individuals to overcome their problems through methods such as counselling, negotiations and legal procedures. In contrast, the latter approaches the problem by changing social attitudes and outlook, particularly in regard to male-female relationships in the community. The Centre studies the factors that affect the relationship within the specific socio-economic and political structure, and uses broad-based methods such as education, consciousness raising, community organisation, political lobbying and dialogues to initiate changes. Indeed,

> It is on the interpretation of 'empowerment' that these two approaches can be compared. The first view looks at empowerment at a more individual level, where women should be self-reliant, make their own decisions; whereas the second approach looks at empowerment at a more organisational/collective level, where structural changes are involved[16].

As a general policy, the Centre rejects any approach which creates total dependence on the organisation or on individual volunteers. Time and again, volunteers are reminded that the WCC is not operating on charity nor subscribing to a welfare mentality. They are reminded not to manipulate the powerful relationship they have with service users. Given the diverse backgrounds of the volunteers, however, the two approaches seem to accommodate everyone's interests. Those who prefer to work with individual women choose the service-oriented approach by using counselling as their working method. On the other hand, those interested in creating structural changes join community out-reach, legal advocacy, and gender sensitisation programmes. Their working methods include negotiation of tasks (especially with public agencies), dialogues, small group discussions, public talks, workshops and seminars.

Activities

Using the two approaches noted above, the WCC has conducted a wide range of activities and provides several types of services to users as well as to the local community. These include:

- direct services, such as counselling support, legal advice, temporary shelter, referrals to obtain 'interim protection orders' and 'protection orders', referral to other organisations or public agencies and general information;

- short-term community outreach programmes such as talks with small group in local communities;
- long-term community partnership programmes such as working on the issue of sexual abuse among children;
- special outreach programmes, such as the programme for Muslim women and the law, looking into the implementation of law and the problems faced by Muslim women;
- advocacy activities, such as legal advocacy and lobbying for policy changes at both local and federal level;
- working with statutory organisations such as hospitals, the police department, the welfare department and the (Islamic) religious authority in order to encourage them to create necessary services, to form a good relationship for the benefit of service users, and to sensitise them to the issues concerned;
- research and publications to gather information to support the services and programmes and to publish simple information for public use;
- developing a resource centre for the organisation as well as for the local community (The Centre is becoming popular as a resource organisation among training institutes and the general public, who want to equip themselves with information and knowledge on women's issues);
- volunteer management programmes—even though the WCC has a good team of qualified staff, volunteers are still assets that need to be sustained and developed. It is important for the organisation to spread the ideals of collective work and volunteerism in the community;
- networking, in order to share information; to develop the Centre's strength and to reciprocate support to organisations with similar interests; and to develop effective and acceptable working relationship with all sectors. Networking is carried out at local, national and international levels.

These have been core activities of the Centre to date. Naturally this will change over time and new activities may be adopted whenever the need arises.

Services

Women who came to the WCC could choose from several types of support, including counselling for emotional support, temporary refuge, legal support, political lobbying, referral to relevant bodies either in the government or NGOs, and, in cases of emergencies, the WCC provides some financial support. It is important to note at this juncture that women themselves have access to a support network—family, friends and their workplace—before they seek assistance from the Centre. Alternatively, they use their personal network simultaneously with assistance from the WCC. Women may also obtain assistance from statutory bodies. From observation, though, one can conclude that those women with access to other support networks, particularly family and friends, seem 'stronger' in dealing with their problems, and are able to sustain their spirit and solve their problems better, compared to those without such a back-up system.

The WCC provides counselling services by trained volunteers and staff. Women who seek these services can choose which language they prefer to communicate in while the WCC tries to accommodate their needs. Those who speak Malay or English have a greater choice of counsellors because most of the latter are fluent in both languages. In most cases, however, women tend to work with volunteers and staff from similar ethnic backgrounds, although cross-cultural counselling does not seem to create any obstacles. Both women and counsellors are well aware of their cultural limitations. On the part of the WCC, the counsellors are always sensitive to the needs of different cultural groups in the community.

In some cases, women come to the WCC at a very late stage in their sufferings, but with high expectations, hoping that their problems can be resolved immediately. After years of living with the problem, they wish that someone can just take it away from them. Sometimes this expectation leads to unrealistic perceptions of the abilities of counsellors and the Centre.

The first thing that a counsellor does is to listen to the women and attend to any immediate needs that they may require, such as accommodation, physical examination, or a police report. The impact of the immediate assistance is crucial. As one woman put it, 'My problem seems lighter after reaching the shelter and talking to the counsellor'[17]. Among other things, the amount of time spent on each individual case depends on the nature and complexity of the problem, the ability of the individual to handle her problem, the support network around her, and the response from the different statutory bodies involved. The helping process goes through different stages. For instance, at the beginning a lot of time is spent identifying the women's problems and ways of resolving them. At this stage, a counsellor may put a lot of emphasis on building the women's self-confidence. At the same time, a counsellor tries to discourage the development of dependency on the counsellor or the Centre. Once this initial period is over, a counsellor plays a supportive role as well as being a source of reference and information.

On an average, a counsellor spends between six months to two years managing a case. A counsellor may also need to support an individual for longer if the person has to go through difficult legal proceeding or other complexities. However, the counsellors remain friends with the women and continue to support them whenever the need arises, even after the case has been officially resolved. Due to the intensity of the helping process, the WCC made it a policy to monitor any negative impacts on volunteer counsellors, and the staff offer support to the counsellors at the same time, to share each other's problems.

SERVICE USERS

The WCC's records show that, from its inception up to 1999, it had assisted as many as 2,410 women (see Table 2.1). This figure refers only to those who came for person-to-person assistance. I personally believe that the WCC has assisted more women because record keeping for the first five years of the WCC was not well organised. Besides, apart from those who came personally to the WCC, the latter also provided counselling services over the telephone. For instance, in 1999 alone, the Centre conducted 1,326 phone-counselling cases compared to 1,368 cases in 1998 and 686 cases in 1997. However, it must be acknowledged that prior to 1997, the records for phone-counselling cases were not properly kept, nor were the services properly organised.

Violence against Women

In terms of assistance sought, women come to the WCC with all kinds of problems but marital conflicts seem to be the most common (see Table 2.1). In most cases, the women claim that their problems arise because of little or no communication with spouses; the presence of a third party (another woman or family intervention); spouses behaving irresponsibly towards the family; financial burdens which caused tension between couples; husbands being addicted to drugs, alcohol, or gambling; and the women's inability to break away from marital relationships. Within the scope of these problems, however, women sometimes mention that they are verbally and emotionally abused as well as mentally tortured by their spouses.

It is interesting to note that, in the first instance, women never identified such problems as violence. They either could not recognise the signs of violence or were simply too buried in denial to admit it. In any case, most women associate violence only with physical violence. In such situations, counsellors who tend to them explain the scope of domestic violence and make them aware of it.

In contrast, those facing sexual harassment and rape have more definite ideas about their problem. In most instances, rape survivors first make a police report and subsequently have a medical examination. In

Table 2.1

Cases handled by the Women's Crisis Centre, 1986–2002

Case Types/Year	'86	'87	'88	'89	'90	'91	'92	'93	'94	'95	'96	'97	'98	'99	'00	'01	'02	Total
Battering	6	10	14	32	43	58	66	51	59	79	59	69	74	69	68	67	71	895
Marital	4	13	26	38	74	87	95	130	81	75	110	64	109	108	75	101	112	1302
Relationship											12	14	20	21	23	13	15	118
Rape		1	1	2	4	7	19	23	7	6	7	5	6	4	2	5	3	102
Sexual Harassment	2		1	4		2		1	2	1	1		2	4	16	7	2	46
Incest												3	4		1	1	4	13
Child Abuse			1		3			4	2			1	1	1	1			14
Legal											27	8	12	23	17	8	29	124
Maintenance												4		2		5		11
Information seeking													5	6	14	5	14	44
Others	1		15	11	36	17	72	59	75	75	14	10	13	22	16	29	17	482
Total	13	25	58	87	160	171	252	268	226	236	230	178	246	260	233	241	267	3151

appropriate cases, legal and other proceedings follow. NGOs intervene only at a later stage when the women concerned need emotional and legal support to face their difficulties. By this stage, however, many survivors lose their enthusiasm and stop pursuing their cases further. As a result, the number of rape survivors who initially came forward to the WCC was very small indeed[18]. Similarly, victims of sexual harassment are discouraged from pursuing their cases because the legal procedures involved are not only tedious but may also backfire. The possible loss of dignity and humiliation resulting from such procedures dishearten many women from putting up a fight, and they disappear from the statistics. Nonetheless, those who seek assistance from the WCC are provided not only with information on the legal status of their cases but, more importantly, they are counselled about other means of handling such violence. This includes learning the technique of confronting the harasser, thereby enhancing self-confidence and sharing the experience with other women or colleagues to build their own strength.

Backgrounds of Service Users

The women who seek help from the WCC come from all socio-economic, ethnic and religious backgrounds. The majority, however, come from lower- to middle-income groups, mainly from the island of Penang. They are mainly married women (working women and housewives) who face marital conflicts and domestic violence; unmarried girls who are pregnant or have been raped; single parents (mostly mothers) who seek support for themselves and their children; migrant workers (domestic servants) who have been raped and/or abused by their employers; male service-users who are husbands or boyfriends and who want the WCC to facilitate reconciliation; those who need legal advice on handling property, who are depressed and lonely, and others. All the service users are either attended to by staff or volunteer counsellors of the WCC. The Centre also makes necessary referrals for those whom it can not assist.

Levels of Suffering

In general, service users come to the WCC at different levels of suffering: in acute cases; situations where there is uncertainty about the problem and the action to be taken; and the stage when legal battles may be sought. These cases are outlined below:

Acute Situation: A large majority of women who seek assistance reach the WCC when they are in a deadlocked situation. They might be physically injured or be running away from life-threatening situations. In many cases they no longer have the resources, information or support to handle their problems themselves. Their self-esteem and self-confidence is low and their sense of self so challenged that they can no longer trust anyone nor any authority. As one woman described her feeling at the critical stage of her crisis, 'I am just an object, I am no longer a human being'[19]. Even when their whole world is falling apart, these women are counselled and informed of their choices and related rights. In many cases, the women themselves decide to take radical action to make a difference in their lives. Often, most of the women have decided on the form of action they want to take when they walk into the WCC's office—cut off the relationship with their abusers totally.

Uncertainty of the Problem and Action: Women who come to the WCC at this level of suffering are usually trying to decide whether they are the cause of the problem or not. They are not sure who is the guilty party. As one woman described it, 'I do everything for him. I take care of the house and the children but he never seems happy with it.' In such cases, self-blame normally occurs. Women at this stage tend to make a lot of excuses for their spouses' abusive action. It is as if they are trying to exhaust all possible reasons before they expose their spouses' abusive actions. They also have many fears and uncertainties, especially of the possible consequences of their actions. For this reason, some of them resigned themselves to the fact that the problem will never go away and that they have to live with it for the rest of their lives.

Legal Battles: Women who need help to face their legal battles usually overcome the first two levels described above. Indeed, for some, they already have the legal proceeding in place before they contact the WCC. For instance, after filing for divorce, they approach the WCC for a legal advisor to proceed with the case. Such women are clear in their approach and have decided on their action, but sometimes subsequent delays and postponements are so long that the women lose the heart and interest to pursue the matter further. In this instance, the WCC provides them with support and motivation to keep their interest and spirit alive.

Seeking Confirmation: At an early stage of conflict resolution, many women phone the WCC to clarify their rights and obtain information on legal procedures. They also seek clarification on the role of different authorities which they might have to face in the process of solving their problems, and search for a second opinion to ensure their problems are real. In many instances, however, these women just want someone to listen to them. They make it very clear that they are not ready to take any action. At best, they are 'just thinking about it'.

Information on the number of cases solved by the WCC is not immediately available but, in general, most service users seem satisfied with the support they obtain from the WCC. As a policy, the Centre encourages service users to stay in touch and to take part in its activities. In some cases, they remain friends of the WCC, and some even become volunteers of the Centre.

Volunteerism

As a non-governmental organisation, the WCC relies heavily on the contribution from its volunteers. To date, it has 30 active volunteers from about 150 fee-paying members and a large pool of support volunteers who are willing to be called upon whenever the need arises. They come from all sorts of educational, social, and ethnic backgrounds and their interest in volunteerism is also varied. Their ages range from those in their twenties to the early seventies. Besides their serious concern with the issue of violence against women, they also have high social, cultural, and religious tolerance, a readiness to get into new ventures, and an ability to differentiate personal from organisational interests. These personal qualities have had some influence on the organisation itself.

As a whole, the group may be divided into those who have been exposed to intellectual debates on women's issues and those who are simply interested in assisting other women. In other words, many members and volunteers do not join the WCC with preconceptions about feminism, empowerment, partnership, gender equality and so on. They come with an open mind and have basic universal human values such as dignity, sincerity, sharing, responsibility, a strong faith in God, and a belief that they must ' . . . give back what God has given you and not hold back'[20].

However, this does not prevent them from changing. The fact that they belong (voluntarily) to women's organisations such as the WCC exposes them to ideas about women's oppression and the need for gender-sensitive practices in daily life. Many of the volunteers are also para-counsellors who support women in crisis. They sometimes accompany the women to different places to obtain services, becoming someone for the latter to lean on. That leaves them with no choice but to take a position over the issues. In other words, they change from simply assisting other women to championing their causes. One volunteer stated, 'I learn many things while in the organisation; the WCC has changed my perspective of life'[21]. Another volunteer, Elizabeth Devaraj, said, 'I change through reading and by being aware of my surrounding, sharing with young people as well as learning from the international arena'[22]. Indeed, there have been several others who have changed their perspective about the position of women in society, particularly in relation to men, and who are not afraid of being labelled a feminist or a social activist. Of course, going through a personal metamorphosis does not make one a social activist, but the desire to change a negative situation into a positive one, to think of others rather than just the well-being of the self, are perhaps the ingredients that turn many WCC volunteers into dedicated campaigners struggling to change women's lives.

At this point, general concern regarding volunteerism recently raised by a small group of volunteers, must be noted: that volunteers are dwindling in number and the frequency of their regular visits to the organisation has fallen significantly. One possibility is that they do not seem to be given a specific duty to fulfil. Save for follow-up cases or clients who require a special approach, most cases are now dealt with directly by the staff. Given the fact that the services provided by WCC have been increasing, it is possible to speculate that the staff are taking over most of the responsibilities and are becoming more efficient. It seems that the need for volunteers declines over the years as the organisation matures, with the staff becoming better qualified and having greater motivation for further commitment.

This does not mean that volunteerism has become irrelevant, however. Though volunteers are fewer in number compared to the early days of the WCC when the Centre was totally dependent on them, volunteers still constitute an integral part of the WCC. The volunteers' concerns are as important as ever to the WCC, and may be outlined briefly as follows:

- How does the organisation use the volunteers?
- Are the jobs given to volunteers meaningful?
- Do the volunteers gain any knowledge or develop from their involvement in the organisation?
- How are volunteers appreciated by the organisation?
- Is there any difference between the older and younger generation of volunteers?

From a short questionnaire given to the volunteers, it may be concluded that many WCC volunteers felt that they were well used. They also benefited from their involvement, particularly by extending their networks and knowledge of the issues involved. They also agreed that they had learnt and appreciated the idea of empowerment. The younger generation of volunteers specifically explained how they should be used, and were more time- and task-oriented than the older volunteers. In other words, they felt that the WCC needs to be more focused about how to use their services. On the other hand, the older generation of volunteers has slowly disengaged itself and chosen to play an advisory role. Notwithstanding all this, however, the questionnaire reminded the organisation not to tax the volunteers to the point of no return. 'The WCC has to have a long-term strategy in managing volunteers and the organisation. They must be considerate and not tax the volunteers'[23]. This feeling was shared by another volunteer who commented that, 'Work in the WCC is challenging and tiring. Leading the WCC even for a year is a big task for me, but I willingly do it because I see what the WCC is doing'[24].

MULTI-ETHNICITY AND CLASS

Volunteerism is not without its problems. In the case of the WCC, it created internal conflicts along the fault lines already present in Malaysian society—those concerning ethnicity. An evaluation report of the Centre stated that,

> The unique character of the WCC volunteers is its multi-raciality and different socio-economic backgrounds still characterised the organisation from history till presently. Their strength lies in that ability to be able to work together despite their great diversities and experiences.[25]

Despite being an asset, multi-ethnic volunteerism produces its own problems. This was exemplified by a crisis in 1993 that shocked the organisation, in which the WCC was accused by some volunteers of being dominated by the middle class and English-educated women, who either refused or were unable to communicate in any other language except English. These individuals also accused the other party of being elitist and intentionally pushing aside the interests of Chinese-educated and Chinese-speaking volunteers. As the conflict developed, a few individuals mobilised both the English and Chinese press to divide the volunteers into ethnic groups, suggesting that this was inevitable. They reminded Malaysians that ethnicity cuts across all aspects of their daily life, even in what seemed to be a united women's front in the WCC. As one journalist put it,

The differences between the English- and Mandarin-educated Chinese are not unique to the WCC. The MCA, the Gerakan, and the DAP (political parties) have their own cultural and class conflicts based on this division.

The English-educated, apart from being middle-class in outlook, tend to have the advantage of being more cosmopolitan. The English-educated Indian, Malay and Chinese generally have more in common than the Chinese-educated have with English-educated Chinese.

The founding mothers of the WCC should have enough theory to anticipate such areas of conflict. It is possible that this group unconsciously used English in their daily discourse on WCC matters[26].

The accusation that the WCC was using English as the medium of communication was partly true. While it is necessary to maintain international linkages, it is also a common practice among organisations in Malaysia today to communicate in a version of local English which may be called 'Manglish' (Malaysian English). This is widely used in daily communication among the general public as well. However, as it turned out, the accusation was only an alibi by a few Chinese-educated volunteers to take over the running of the WCC. The group had been planning to seize control at the Annual General Meeting of 1993, which caught the rest of the volunteers by surprise. Apparently the group had been lobbying for support by bringing in an influx of Chinese members into the WCC since early 1993, without the management committee being aware of this strategy. However, the delay by the General Committee to approve their membership (due to other duties) turned out to be a functional inefficiency, because the threat of the takeover was quite real. This was apparent during the Eighth Annual General Meeting the following year, when the 'Chinese-educated group' contested every position in the General Committee. It managed to win the post of President, but then the whole year proved to be the most difficult one for the WCC as other members of the General Committee and the President were at odds with each other. The President was accused by the Committee of playing up the WCC's ethnic issues in the press and was asked to resign. After she refused, the matter was brought to an extraordinary general meeting in October that year when the President was ousted with a vote of no confidence.

In a sense, this conflict was a reminder to the organisation of the reality of Malaysian society. The diversity in the backgrounds and ethnicity of the volunteers, commonly regarded as the strength of the organisation, now became its greatest challenge. Ethnic division persistently lurks in the background and haunts the most unsuspecting victims. The WCC has always been aware of the problem, but to avoid a recurrence of the 1993 crisis, it has become more vigilant by creating a degree of ethnic balance in its General Committee and staff. It also scrutinises and restricts new members to those who show great interest and commitment to women's causes.

Apart from the above problems of ethnicity, the WCC has been identified as an organisation which is run by the educated urban middle-class. This is an image which the Centre has had to live with for some time to come as the majority of active volunteers are middle-class. However, they are highly motivated and committed to the cause compared to other classes. Indeed, most social movements and voluntary groups in Malaysia are led or supported by the middle class. The WCC is aware of the implications of this image problem and in response, has always taken cognisance of class issues whenever it organises a function, and so far it has not organised grand elitist functions which alienate the lower classes.

The fact that the WCC has an urban location is perhaps an issue as well. Although Penang is quite urbanised, rural-urban demarcations still divide the population and differentiate their access to services. This occurs along ethnic lines since the majority of the Chinese population live in urban areas, the Malays live in rural areas, and the Indians are found in both areas. To maintain multi-ethnic services, the WCC endeavours to reach out to all groups equally.

LEGAL ADVOCACY AND EMPOWERMENT

In the beginning of the struggle, women's organisations in Malaysia, including the WCC, had access to many legal provisions to carry out their work. These included the Penal Code, the Law Reform (Marriage and Divorce) Act, the Syariah Law (for Muslims) Evidence Act and Special Relief Act. These provisions were generally found to be inadequate as there was no sufficient legal provision specific to the needs of violated women. Consequently, at a workshop in 1985, the women's group which had formed a Joint Action Group conceptualised the idea and lobbied for an effective legal provision specific to cases of violence against women[27]. The matter was taken up by the NCWO, which submitted a memorandum on the subject to the Minister of Justice that same year. The immediate demand was for the government to enact a law against domestic violence to protect women and enhance the development of a more equitable gender relationship. By 1989, a joint committee was set up to examine the proposed Act, consisting of the Joint Action Group, the NCWO, the Bar Council, the HAWA, the Department of Social Welfare, the Ministry of Health, the Police and the Islamic Affairs Department. The committee proposed amendments to the Penal Code and other relevant acts on rape, and proposed a Domestic Violence Act in 1990, which classified domestic violence as a crime. This was forwarded to the Attorney General's office. As it was originally formulated, the Act was ' ... designed to grant both civil and criminal remedies for victims of domestic violence, irrespective of religious or cultural consideration'[28]. The intention was to include family problems, such as divorce and custody, while at the same time protecting women from violent acts by their abusers. However, such a proposal turned it into a 'quasi-civil' law, whereas the Malaysian legal system separates civil from criminal law. To make it relevant for the protection of women, the women's organisations had to agree with the Attorney General's office for the Act to be attached to the Criminal Procedure of the Penal Code (the state's criminal law), so that domestic violence offences would be classified as criminal actions[29].

The proposal was subsequently formulated into a legislative bill and, after several delays, was finally passed by Parliament on 12 May 1994 as the Domestic Violence Act 1994[30]. The approval of the Act by Parliament was a big step in combating violence against women. Malaysia became the first country in South-East Asia, and the first Muslim country, that had enacted a law to protect and liberate women from sexual crimes. The general intention of the Act was to provide immediate relief, to ensure the safety of the victims and to expedite and simplify the reporting and injunction procedures. When the Act was announced, however, women's groups noticed some serious flaws, such as the lack of penalties and enforcement procedures (for example, victims have to rely on the Penal Code to proceed with their cases). There were also several instances where domestic violence cases were classified as 'non-seizable' offences—that is, where offenders could not be reprimanded immediately upon report. The women's organisations therefore called for ' ... additional regulations to strengthen the implementation of the Act like specific form to make report and procedures on investigating the case'[31]. By June 1996, after an 11-year struggle, the Act was implemented with some procedural matters rectified.

According to the Act (Malaysia), domestic violence is defined as any one or more of the following actions:

- wilfully or knowingly placing, or attempting to place, the victim in fear of physical injury;
- causing physical injury to the victim by such acts which are known or should be known to result in physical injury;
- compelling the victim by force or threat to engage in any conduct or act, sexual or otherwise, from which the victim has the right to abstain;
- confining or detaining the victim against the victim's will;
- causing mischief, destruction, or damage to property with intent to cause, or knowing that it is likely to cause, distress or annoyance to the victim[32].

Even though the majority of the victims of domestic violence are women, the Act was not created with the intention of becoming a women's charter. Indeed, the Act is supposed to protect all victims, male or female, adult or children. The actions listed above do not single out a particular perpetrator, so long as they are carried out by a person towards 'his or her spouses, his or her former spouses, a child, an incapacitated adult or any other member of the family'[33].

Women's organisations, including the WCC, took immediate steps to monitor the Act as soon as it was implemented[34]. They then realised that some government agencies handling abused women were indifferent to the victims and some victims had to wait too long to receive their protection orders[35]. Besides monitoring the Act, the WCC and other women's organisations were also involved in promoting awareness and understanding of the Act among the general public, particularly among women. The strategies used included public fora and effective use of the media. At the same time, they tried to sensitise government agencies such as the police departments, social welfare departments, the hospitals and the courts to the problems of abused women.

Among the women's organisations, however, it was the WCC, through its legal reform sub-committee, which took the lead in strengthening the Domestic Violence Act by drawing a memorandum to review it. Twenty points were raised with regard to its implementation, and include, among other things: clarifying the duties of public officers; recognising the victims' ability to appear in court on her own; broadening the definition of domestic violence under the Domestic Violence

Act; eliminating the requirement of obtaining an order to investi-
gate for non-seizable offences before obtaining an Interim Protection
Order; and improving access to exclusive possession for protected
persons.

The memorandum was supported by 21 other women's groups and
sent to the prime minister's department in December 1998. A revised
copy was later sent to the Women's Affairs section of the Ministry of
Unity and Social Development in March 1999 (the latest reshuffling
of government ministries had changed the location of women's affairs
to the prime minister's department)[36]. To date, the government has
only agreed to look into the matter. While there is no doubt that legal
measures are effective in protecting women and promoting social justice which may finally lead to gender-equality practices, the exercise
itself took a great deal of time. But for the dedication of the volunteers of women's organisations such as the WCC, it may not have
materialised.

Apart from the struggle for Domestic Violence Act, the WCC also
made significant contributions to the formulation of the Child Bill 2000
and the current proposal for a Bill on Sexual Harassment.

THE WCC AND GOVERNMENT AGENCIES

Apart from the government legislating a legal framework in which
women's organisations can operate, some of its agencies are directly
involved in solving women's problems. I will highlight some of the
experiences encountered while working with some of the government
agencies and the importance of lobbying for political support in order
to change prevailing ideas about women and empowerment.

In most cases, the focus and services of government agencies for
women's issues are new. At the time when the WCC was established,
many of these agencies did not even feel the need to highlight women's
problems and concerns. The stereotypical perception of women, especially of those who were abused, was so opaque that it seemed almost
impossible for organisations such as the WCC to make a breakthrough.
To some extent, the perception of government agencies represented
the erroneous thinking on women's issues prevalent in the community
at large[37]. Indeed, it must have been very difficult for the agencies to
change their male-oriented framework and be sensitive to women's
needs or at least to be 'gender-neutral'.

The goal of the WCC's relationship with government agencies was to develop a partnership with them to change their outlook and to create a more women-sensitive social environment. The WCC began by informing government agencies of its existence. Volunteers deemed 'politically correct' were carefully selected to visit these agencies and introduce them to the WCC. In general, the volunteers were received politely. Problems only arose when volunteers either started to refer women's cases to these agencies, or accompanied them to the agencies to settle their problems. At the beginning, there was much tension between volunteers and the agencies concerned as the latter were either unexposed to the issues, or were simply determined to brush them aside and avoid them. The volunteers, on the other hand, were too eager to 'reform' everyone on their path, thus getting into unnecessary confrontations. Further, the volunteers had yet to establish a personal rapport with the agencies. While this was happening at the local level, women's groups were lobbying for changes with the headquarters of government departments in Kuala Lumpur. With the exception of the Islamic religious department, whose authority is confined to state level, the headquarters of government agencies seemed more receptive to the issues and even took part in national training programmes organised by the women's groups[38]. The headquarters later sent directives to their branches at state level directing them either to take part in similar training programmes or to support women's issues. This bureaucratic support for women's causes seemed to work to the WCC's advantage. For instance, by the beginning of the 1990s, the agencies began to take part in the Centre's activities, such as seminars and workshops. By the mid-1990s, the Centre had managed to develop a more concrete relationship with them. The best example of this was the launching of two long-term projects with the Hospital and the Education Departments at the state level.

Partnership with Hospitals

In 1995 the Centre began negotiating with the Health Department to develop an integrated service within the hospital framework. The objective was to reduce the trauma faced by abused victims. In normal circumstances, women had to wait long hours at hospital emergency or the out-patient departments before they were attended to. They were also open to scrutiny by other people around them while waiting, and once the medical examination began, they could be directed to several different departments within the hospital. The whole experience added to the trauma they had already experienced through being abused. The WCC therefore suggested that the hospital provide a specific room where the victims could rest and undergo medical examinations. Surprisingly, the Health Department was very responsive to the idea, and in May 1996, the One-Stop Crisis Centre (OSCC) at the General Hospital in Penang was officially inaugurated by the Minister of Health.

Even though the OSCC was the second one in the country (the first was established at the Kuala Lumpur General Hospital), it was strategised for wide media coverage. In his speech the Minister mentioned the need for such centres at all government hospitals in the country, and soon after the launch, all government hospitals in the country received a directive to start such centres. The WCC continued to sustain the momentum by holding a national seminar on the OSCC in August the same year, with participants drawn from all over the country. The organisation also developed a training programme for personnel in charge of the OSCC at hospitals outside Penang. This was followed by the publication of a manual to assist and sustain the work at the OSCCs. As a long-term working relationship, the WCC and the hospital agreed to conduct a review of the programme twice a year. In the final analysis, the WCC gained some ground through this programme, not only because it was well received, but also because it created a sense of completion to the Centre's endeavours. Sustaining the work of the OSCC means sustaining interest on the issue of violence against women. At the same time, the victims of abuse are treated with respect and dignity.

Partnership with Schools

While women's organisations achieved major breakthroughs in their work with adult women, the incidence of child sexual abuse required equal, if not more, attention[39]. The WCC took on the issue by creating an awareness programme with primary school children and teachers. In the programme, school children were informed of their rights not to be abused and teachers were encouraged to take proactive roles in handling the issue. The programme received support from the State Assembly in charge of education and the Education Department of Penang. The main feature of this programme was the method through which the issue was presented to the children. The WCC used a theatre forum method which encouraged children to participate in dialogues. The children were also provided with booklets which explained their rights in simple terms. The fact that a WCC member who was also a children's theatre specialist created the programme probably explains its success. It received positive and wide local and national media coverage. The programme is now developing a manual for teachers which will include secondary school children to ensure wider coverage.

Both these activities illustrate how the WCC empowered itself as an organisation through building partnerships with government agencies. Furthermore, the media was also instrumental in promoting the WCC's ideas and has highlighted our capacity to tackle violence against women. The working strategy of the WCC can be outlined as follows:

- recognising the capacity of government agencies both at the state and federal level;
- developing personal relationships at the local level, especially with front-line staff;
- lobbying individual politicians for support;
- ensuring that each programme receives good media coverage;

- developing a support system or network to ensure the smooth running of programmes;
- providing written reference material;
- sustaining the momentum of interest to further its plans.

However, the present partnership with government agencies may not last very long if there is no real commitment to the issues. The challenge now is to find ways of sustaining their interest and sensitising them fully to the importance of the programmes. Perhaps the time has come for the WCC to consider itself an equal partner to the government, and move into the area of policy-making with the government.

IMPACT OF THE WCC

As noted earlier, the development of the WCC as a women's organisation was greatly supported by the timing of its creation. By then, both the public and the authorities were already exposed to women's issues. While drawing strength from the formation of other women's organisations, the WCC brought the issue into the local community to gain its support and confidence. Together with other women's organisations, the WCC has created an impact on the local community and managed to change attitudes towards violence against women by emphasising the following concerns:

Redefining Violence Against Women as an Aspect of Women's Oppression: For instance, domestic violence, rape, and sexual harassment are seen as a result of prevailing social values and the social structure[40]. In a patriarchal society like Malaysia, power is still concentrated in men's hands. The women's organisations therefore insisted that the imbalance of power in male-female relationships is the cause of violence. Understandably, they encountered much resistance at first. For instance, the women's groups were accused of aping Western feminist movements and challenging men's power was the direct result of Western influence.

Transforming the Issues of Domestic Violence from Private to Public Spheres: Domestic violence is not a problem between two individuals within their limited environment. It is a manifestation of larger problems in society, between the powerful and the powerless.

Recognising the Range of Damage Resulting from Acts of Violence Against Women: The community was informed that acts of violence are not limited to the person violated. They also affect others around them, such as their children, parents and other close relations. It does not only leave the victims physically bruised, but causes mental and psychological damage as well as threatens their economic productivity. In other words, community members were encouraged to see the result of violence beyond mere physical injuries.

Overcoming these issues was not achieved in a short period. The task of convincing the public is in steady progress. If at first the WCC was blamed for causing broken marriages, we now hear less of it. Indeed, like other women's organisations in Malaysia, the WCC seems to have been accepted. It can at least claim to have achieved a civil relationship with agencies that were uncertain of their positions on the issue of violence against women. In the words of a President of the WCC,

> The WCC is known not only in Penang, but both within and outside the country. For example, our presence is recognised by the Police, Hospital and the Religious Departments. Often, hospital authorities have contacted us to refer rape survivors to our counsellors. The Religious Department is paying more attention to women clients who are accompanied by WCC case counsellors. Thus after seven years in existence, we are now being recognised as a body with useful functions[41].

CONCLUSION

The WCC's 17-year struggle to uphold women's rights and to assist women who were abused has not been futile. It has made an impact in both the state of Penang as well as in Malaysia as a whole. The organisation has made remarkable achievements to empower itself, its volunteers and service users. In conclusion, we can draw several lessons on empowerment from the experience of the WCC. First, a major factor in the WCC's success has been the existence of a core group of highly dedicated volunteers. Even though most of them work full-time in highly demanding jobs as lawyers, academics, or businesswomen, they give their full support to the WCC by putting in extra hours after work, including weekends. In some cases, they even take special leave from their jobs to conduct programmes or attend WCC activities. Second, contrary to the common belief that ethnic differences may cause tensions and conflict at work, particularly in voluntary work, the core group of volunteers has managed to overcome ethnic differences, and focused on a single issue of common interest—women's well-being.

But the dedication of volunteers would not be sufficient to promote an organisation without proper governance. In this respect, the WCC found a formula in collective leadership and decision-making. By instituting a system of rotating office-bearers and a system of checks and balances in the decision-making process, it has been ensured no one 'owns' the organisation. This translates into efficient development and management of programmes, staff and finance. This is also made possible by a policy of not only hiring qualified and dedicated people as staff, but also hiring those who are committed to the women's agenda.

The operating environment must also be compatible with the goals and objectives of the women's struggle. The WCC is blessed in this sense, because both the community and the government are quite amenable to its requests and needs. Community members, for instance, contribute regularly to WCC activities, both in cash and in kind. At the same time, the community in Penang and in Malaysia in general is not aggressive towards women in the sense of preventing women from expressing themselves freely or hindering their activities. Very seldom is extreme action to control women on religious, cultural, or ethnic grounds entertained by the community.

The government, on the other hand, is open to providing space for the Centre to develop and promote its activities and services. Most crucial in this area is perhaps the formulation and implementation of the Domestic Violence Act, 1994. Even though there are shortcomings in the Act, the fact that the women's struggle is recognised and translated into law provides tremendous space for women to make their voices heard. The government is also responsive towards women's issues at national and international levels. While accepting international recommendations by bodies such as the United Nations, government agencies are willing to enter into dialogue and direct partnerships with women's organisations, but without dominating them. Indeed, the independence of women's organisations such as the WCC to pursue their goals is crucial for their success.

While all this indicates a high degree of success, it must be noted that the WCC still has a much room for improvement. Given the present favourable conditions however, the WCC should be able to improve in areas such as documentation processing, reaching out to more women in a broader geographical range, and focussing better on areas where service procedures are not well established, such as rape, incest and sexual harassment. In the final analysis, the WCC does provide several positive lessons on empowering women. However, it may be cautioned that its relative success has to be seen in its proper context. It is quite clear that the WCC's dedication and struggle bear fruit within a particular Malaysian socio-political conjuncture. Could this not be repeated in other contexts as well?

NOTES AND REFERENCES

1. Unless otherwise stated, all the data on Malaysia in this section is taken from two sources: the Government of Malaysia, *The Eighth Malaysia Plan 2001-2005* and *The Seventh Malaysia Plan 1996-2000* (Kuala Lumpur, Percetakan Nasional Malaysia Berhad, 2001;1996) and the Government of Malaysia, *Mid-Term Review of the Seventh Malaysia Plan 1996-2000* (Kuala Lumpur, Percetakan Nasional Malaysia Berhad, 1999).
2. Examples may be cited of the following legislations: Women and Girls Protection Acts 1973, The Law Reform (Marriage and Divorce) Act 1976, the Islamic Family Law Enactment and the Domestic Violence Act 1994.
3. The composition of women workers in various types of occupation in 1995 is as follows:

Occupation category	Male (%)	Female (%)
Professional, technical and related workers	8.9	13.5*
Administrative and managerial workers	4.7	1.9
Clerical and related workers	7.1	17.5
Sales and related workers	11.1	12.1
Service workers	9.5	17.4
Agriculture workers	20.4	14.8
Production and related workers	38.4	22.6
Total	100	100

*A large proportion of the women in this category are school teachers and nurses.
Source: Government of Malaysia, *Seventh Malaysia Plan 1996–2000*, Kuala Lumpur, Percetakan Nasional Malaysia Berhad, 1996, p. 624.

4. In the electronic industries, for instance, women were paid 82.7 per cent of male wages in 1990. This has increased to 92.5 per cent in 1995.

5. The secretariat was later transferred to the Ministry of National Unity and Social Development.

6. The Sixth and Seventh Malaysia Plans (1991–1995 and 1996–2000 respectively) each have a chapter on 'Women in Development'.

7. Statement by the Minister of Human Resources, as quoted in the *New Straits Times*, 28 January 2000, p. 6.

8. By 1994, the organisation had 72 affiliates.

9. The Women's Aid Organisation (WAO) was established in 1982 in Petaling Jaya Selangor, near the capital city Kuala Lumpur. A newspaper called *The Malay Mail*, which published a report about a women's shelter, immediately received a call from a distressed woman. See *Annual Report*, Women's Aid Organisation, 1982–1983.

10. The groups that set up the Joint Action Group (JAG) were: the Women's Aid Organisation; the University Women's Association; the Association of Women Lawyers; the Malaysian Trade Union Congress (women's section); and the Selangor Consumer Association. The workshop was held from 23–24 March 1985. Few volunteers from the WCC attended the meeting, and became part of the caucus. The atmosphere was full of hope and the women were committed to change their situation and overcome violence.

11. For example: i) Persatuan Sahabat Wanita Selangor (PAWS) works specifically with lower-income women, ii) Women for Women Association (WOW) provides policy inputs affecting the female workforce, iii) Asia Pacific Forum on Women and Law (APWLD) focuses on making law an effective instrument for empowerment and promotion of the basic concept of human rights for women.

12. In Malaysia, non-business organisations are required by law to register with the Registrar of Societies. The registration process normally takes between six months to two years.

13. The main source of funds since 1990 has been the Humanistic Institute for Co-operation with Developing Countries (HIVOS), from Holland.

14. See Rajesh Tandon, 'Board Games: Governance and Accountability in NGOs', in Michael Edwards and David Hulme (eds.), *Non-Governmental Organisations—Performance and Accountability* (London: Earthscan, 1995 pp. 41–50). The quotation is taken from p. 42.

15. Loh Cheng Kooi and Ratna Saptari, *Evaluation Report Prepared for HIVOS*, Penang, 1994.

16. ibid., p. 10.

17. An Indonesian service user's description of her experience, noted from the WCC case file, 1998.

18. Research by the All Women's Action Society indicates that 80 per cent of rape cases were dropped before the accused could be charged. The number of reported incidents, however, increased tremendously. Police report shows

that there were 879 cases of rape in 1993. This has increased to 1489 by 1998. See All Women's Action Society, 'Working Together Towards Better Services for Rape Survivors', Draft Report, Kuala Lumpur: 7 December, 1999. See also the reports in *The New Straits Times*, 8 December 1999.

19. This statement was related to me by one of the WCC counsellors. The woman was not certain whether anyone would help her when she first approached the counsellor. At that point, she did not trust any authority, after suffering abuse for about 15 years. She has now divorced her husband and, according to the counsellor who is still in touch with her after working on the case for three years, she is making progress in her life.

20. Statement by Miki Goh Hoalim, who is one of the WCC founder members, and still a practising lawyer at age 71. Currently, she is the legal and financial advisor to the WCC.

21. Statement by Jenny, a homemaker who is dedicated to helping service users at the WCC. She willingly took a counselling training course in order to improve her helping skills. She shared this opinion with us on 20 September 1999, during a volunteer camp.

22. Elizabeth is a retired school teacher, nearly 70 years old, who has raised a family of activists. Her husband and children are very active in politics and social justice issues. I observed the changes in her ideas and orientation from the time she joined the WCC as a volunteer in 1985.

23. Statement by Miki Goh Hoalim, 20 November 1999.

24. Statement by Badariyah, President of the WCC (1997), 20 November 1999.

25. Loh Cheng Kui and Ratna Saptari, p. 4

26. K. Gurunathan, 'Crisis at the Crisis Centre', *The Sun*, 29 October 1993.

27. Joint Action Group, 1986, proceeding of a workshop-cum-exhibition on 'Violence Against Women', 23–24 March 1985, Appendix C, pp. 73–79.

28. Herbert, Laura, 'Monitoring the Domestic Violence Act', Research paper prepared for Women's Aid Organisation, Kuala Lumpur, 1997.

29. Ibid.

30. *The New Sunday Times*, 15 May 1994. Besides the Domestic Violence Act, Parliament also passed the Married Women (Amendment) Bill, 1994.

31. Statement made by the Joint Action Group, which was supported by many women organisations including the WCC, *The New Straits Times*, 14 May 1994.

32. Laws of Malaysia, Domestic Violence Act, 1994 (Act 521).

33. Ibid.

34. The monitoring project was led by the Woman's Aid Organisation. It was divided into three stages: Stage 1(1996–97) analysed the Act by documenting the first-hand experience of women; Stage 2 (1998) focused on advocacy and public education; Stage 3 (1999–July 2000) documented cases in Selangor, Kuala Lumpur, and Penang.

35. *The Sun*, 11 October 1999.

36. See Legal Reform Sub-Committee of Women's Crisis Centre, 'Memorandum of Review and Proposals for Amendments of The Domestic Violence Act 1994', Penang, March 1999.

37. In 1984, when the idea of setting up a crisis centre in Penang was mooted, a colleague and I went to several government departments to collect statistics on domestic violence and rape. This was when we realised how rampant the stereotypical attitudes described in the literature on women were.

38. The first integrated training programme was organised by the National Council of Women Organisation (NCWO) on the theme of handling rape survivors. Government departments such the Police, the Hospital and the Social Welfare Department took part in the programme.

39. A recent report based on research undertaken by the All Women's Action Society confirms the fact that rape inflicted on children below 16 years of age has doubled in the last five years (*The New Straits Times*, 8 December 1999).

40. Liz Kelly, *Towards Integrated Community Response*, London: Children and Women Study Unit, University of North London, 1993.

41. Women's Crisis Centre, Annual Report (President's Report), 1992, p. 6.

3

The Satyodaya Centre: Empowering Tamil Estate Workers in Sri Lanka

Muthuvadivoo Sinnathamby

Today Satyodaya Centre is a mixed community of inter-ethnic, inter-religious, inter-linguistic, inter-generational, inter-class people living and working together. . . . .Satyodaya's work includes community organisation; co-ordinating income-generating projects; self-employment schemes; vocational training; reading rooms/clubs; health and nutrition programmes; and food-for-work (Shramadana) *programmes. This proactive community is even more startling in a country where nearly 40,000 of its 17 million people have been killed in an 11-year civil war drawn on ethnic lines. . . if here, why not elsewhere?*

Elizabeth O'Keele, Jesuit Refugee Service Centre, 1994

INTRODUCTION

I was born on a tea estate in Sri Lanka, where my father was employed. In a long career of nearly 40 years, he had served on three estates located in different tea-growing areas of Sri Lanka. Since he was a resident officer, we lived with him on these estates, and this provided me with ample opportunity to observe and experience the living and working conditions of the estate workers, which were harsh and even inhuman at times. Therefore, it was only natural that when I was selected by the Commonwealth Foundation to write about 'Lessons in Empowerment' from the NGO sector in Sri Lanka, I chose to write about an organisation that has been working among these people for more than 25 years.[1] Initially, I had wanted to write about the experience of a few selected NGOs in the field. After some preliminary work, however, I realised that the NGOs I had selected for study were so different in size, structure, objectives and orientation, that it was difficult to write anything meaningful about all of them. In the end, I decided to concentrate on the activities of just one of them, namely the Satyodaya Centre for Social Research and Encounter (henceforth 'Satyodaya', literally the 'Dawn of Truth'). My association with this organisation goes back to 1974, the year I had returned to Sri Lanka from England after my postgraduate studies.

Around this time, Sri Lanka was in the grip of a serious economic crisis, caused primarily by an acute shortage of foreign exchange which made it difficult to import even basic food items and clothing. The oil price hike of late 1973, the worldwide escalation of food grain prices, and the long and continued drought conditions which affected domestic food production, had all combined to create a near-famine situation in the country. While it was true that the food shortages affected the entire population of the country, it was, by and large, the estate workers who were the most affected. This was because their production activities, unlike those of the rural peasants (who were primarily engaged in subsistence farming), were oriented entirely towards the production of export crops. They were totally dependent on imported food grains for their subsistence and, therefore, the import cuts and price increases affected them adversely. The condition of these workers was further aggravated by certain government policies of the time.

In the aftermath of the Youth Insurgency of April 1971, the government hurriedly introduced a Land Reform Act under which privately owned lands exceeding 20 hectares were taken over. Since it was mostly estate lands that exceeded 20 hectares, much of the land taken over under this Act happened to be under tea and rubber cultivation. The management structures introduced on these lands after their takeover had adverse consequences for the Tamil resident workers. The prevailing drought conditions and food shortage, in combination with the takeover of estate lands and the new management structures introduced to manage them, resulted in unemployment and underemployment, while ethnically motivated attacks and eviction from estate lands resulted in homelessness and induced a feeling of insecurity among the Tamils. According to some sources, there were also a number of deaths among the Tamils admitted to state hospitals for treatment, because of their anaemic condition. These were, however, not officially recorded as deaths due to anaemia.

These unfortunate developments gave rise to the emergence of a number of NGOs in the plantation areas that began to work among these people. But these NGOs tended to work in isolation, oblivious of what the other organisations were doing. The Satyodaya Centre that had just been established in Kandy (in the Central Province) convened a meeting of 22 such groups in October 1974 to discuss the situation in the plantation areas. As the representative of a small organisation that had been formed only a few months ago for the promotion of education among the children of the plantation workers, I was chosen as the Secretary for this meeting. This marked the beginning of my association with Satyodaya, and my subsequent involvement in NGO activities among estate workers in general.

Satyodaya's work with estate workers cannot be understood without a clear understanding of the Sri Lankan economy, polity and society, and the historical background and the current problems faced by the estate Tamil community. The next few pages are devoted to explaining these conditions.

PART I: THE ECONOMY, SOCIETY, AND POLITY OF SRI LANKA

The People of Sri Lanka

Sri Lanka, an island in the Indian Ocean spanning just over 400 km from north to south and about 200 km from east to west, is situated just off the southern tip of India. Because of its size, shape, and location, it has been referred to as the 'teardrop of India'. Known to travellers from ancient times for its precious stones, spices, elephants and scenic beauty, Sri Lanka is well-documented in the tales of the ancient Greeks, Romans, Arabs and Chinese (NARESA 1991). Its location, straddling the sea routes between the East and West, made it a prize for invaders from countries such as India, Portugal, Holland and Britain, who brought their varied cultural and political influences to bear on Sri Lanka. Historically, Sri Lanka's proximity to the Indian subcontinent[2] also brought it under the cultural, religious, linguistic and political influence of India. The country's 'ethnic structures have been predominantly influenced by the processes of colonisation, conquests and conversions from India over several centuries' (Phadnis 1990). As a result, the present multi-ethnic configuration of the Sri Lankan population owes much to Indian influences, with the exceptions of the Arab migrant traders or Moors who settled in the island at various times, forming a large part of the Muslim community; the Malays, brought as soldiers by the Dutch; and the Burghers, a community of Eurasian and European descent.

Ethnic and Religious Composition of the Population

The most critical division of the country's population is between the majority Sinhalese, who form about 75 per cent of the total population, and the Tamils, who consist of Sri Lankan or 'traditional' Tamils[3] who had settled on the island several centuries ago, as well as Tamils of recent Indian origin, the majority of whom are either estate or plantation workers. Together, the Tamils account for nearly 18 per cent of the population. The balance is constituted by Moors and other minorities. The religious divisions, too, roughly correspond to the above proportions. Most Sinhalese are Buddhist, most Tamils are Hindu, and most Moors are Muslim, but there are also Christian Sinhalese and Tamils (Warnapala and Woodsworth 1987).

The Economy

Agriculture, with its two sub-sectors of peasant small holdings and plantations, remains an important lead sector in the economy of Sri Lanka. It contributes around 25 per cent of the Gross Domestic Product (GDP) and employs a little over half the labour force. It has made a substantial contribution to export earnings and, until recently, to government revenue as well. Export crops, principally tea, rubber and coconut, are Sri Lanka's main source of export earnings. In recent years, however, garment exports, tourism and expatriate worker remittances have also increased their contribution to the export earnings of the country.

Around 42 per cent of the arable land area is already under cultivation. Half the existing forest area is potentially suitable for agriculture. However, for ecological reasons, this forest cover cannot be converted into farmlands. Land, the most important factor of production for any form of agriculture, is therefore a scarce resource in Sri Lanka. But in spite of the limited land area, the cultivation of a wide range of crops has been possible because of variations in precipitation, topography and soil.

Sri Lanka is one of the first developing countries to have adopted a programme of economic liberalisation, viz. the structural adjustment programmes (SAPs). In fact, it had introduced this programme three years before the World Bank embarked upon its structural adjustment loans in the 1980s. Sri Lanka can therefore be considered a pioneer in the implementation of SAP policies in the South Asian region. This change of policy, from one of controlled economy pursued since the early 1960s, was an attempt by the then government to keep the country in line with the most successful Asian economies, and thereafter raise it to the status National Identity Card (NIC) holder by the turn of the 20th century. The new strategy sought to increase the role of markets and the private sector by reducing or eliminating restrictions on pricing, investment and external trade and payments. This strategy has been pursued by all subsequent governments as well.

The growth rate of the economy improved significantly after 1977. It almost doubled during the next five to six years, but began to slacken around the mid-1980s. The ethnic riots of 1983, the consequent civil disturbances in the country and the gradual withdrawal of the massive public investment programme on infrastructure construction were mainly responsible for this. Despite the improved growth rate experienced in the early part of the reform programme, macro-economic imbalances have been a major source of worry throughout the post-reform period. Factors such as trade liberalisation, currency devaluation (floating of the currency), excessive budget deficits and balance of payments disequilibrium, have induced high inflationary pressures, causing real incomes to fall. Income distribution, which had improved for the two decades since 1953, worsened with the introduction of liberal market policies. The distribution of income had shifted in favour of the urban sector, while the rural sector, constituted by a large majority of the population, suffered a loss in its share. The shift in government expenditure away from welfare towards large infrastructure projects was the obvious reason for this. Consequently, about a quarter of the population continued to remain poor despite gains in economic growth.

Sri Lanka had a widespread state welfare structure in place at the time of the introduction of the SAP, which included a network of subsidised rice, flour distribution and rationing, free education, poor relief and subsidised or free medical care. This helped the country achieve a fairly high quality of life in comparison with its low per capita income. The annual growth in GDP, together with relatively low population growth, raised Sri Lanka's per capita GDP to US$ 856 in 2000 from US$ 825 in 1999. Consequently, the country's position in the international classification moved further up within the lower middle income category (which includes countries with a per capita income in the range of US$ 795–3125). Sri Lanka will have to maintain an annual growth rate of 7–8 per cent over the next few years to move further upwards. However, the brunt of fiscal adjustments that had been made conditional for continued World Bank/IMF assistance is borne by capital expenditure, and this is likely to affect economic growth adversely in the next few years. The growth of investment is already sluggish. Although there has been a gradual increase in private investment in the last few years, this is far from adequate to compensate for the decline in public investment.

Governance

Some of the SAP conditions such as devaluation (floating of the rupee), reduction in budget deficits (as the bulk of government cuts in spending fell on socially productive expenditure on education, health and social security), the reduction of subsidies and the sale of public enterprises, have met with resistance from sections of the community that suffered from a fall in real wages and income, and became impoverished as a result of such policies. The government, in an attempt to create the right political and social conditions for accelerated growth, introduced various social mobilisation programmes such as the *gam udawas* (village awakening), a massive rural housing programme and 'mobile secretariats' where high-ranking government officials were required to travel to outlying areas to solve local problems. As these projects were introduced without independent technical assessment, with quick results being the only justification, they turned out to be costly exercises. Lack of accountability and transparency, corruption, negligence, waste and authoritarianism in governance became the order of the day (Abeyasekara and Bastian 1993). This was simply 'bad governance' as defined by the World Bank (1992).

Ethnic Conflict and the Civil War

Sri Lanka is home to a number of ethnic and religious communities who had lived in harmony for centuries without open conflicts, despite the dynastic wars among ruling houses from time to time. During British rule, however, ethnic consciousness acquired pronounced expression and the major ethnic communities in Sri Lanka drifted apart from one another through the prevalent competitive economic and political processes. What started as competition for public service positions, particularly among the educated middle-class Sinhalese and Tamils, later turned into community rivalry. The Jaffna peninsula, where the Sri Lanka Tamil community is heavily concentrated, was the first to benefit from schools opened by Christian missionaries belonging to different denominations. It gave the Sri Lanka Tamils the opportunity to acquire an English education earlier than the other communities and thereby enjoy an advantage over others in the competition for public service positions. Over time, the Sinhalese began to feel that the Tamils were disproportionately represented in the expanding public service under British rule. Similarly, after Independence there was a widespread belief among the Tamils that under the parliamentary democratic system, the overwhelming Sinhala majority used its power to divert the scarce resources available to the country predominantly to serve the interests of the majority community (Gunasinghe 1987). From 1930 onwards, under the state-sponsored land resettlement schemes, large numbers of Sinhala families from the densely populated south-western quarter of Sri Lanka were resettled in the relatively unpopulated dry zone areas. Some of these Sinhala settlements extended to the very fringe of the Tamil settlements in the Jaffna Peninsula. When such new settlements began to seriously affect the ethnic composition of the population of these areas, Tamils in the adjacent areas became agitated, fearing that it would have serious consequences on their parliamentary representation. This also gave rise to the later Tamil claims of a traditional homeland in these areas and the accusation that the government was attempting to colonise these areas with the Sinhalese and thereby change their ethnic composition permanently, with the objective of weakening the Tamils. This became a major grievance of the Tamils in the succeeding period.

Relations between the two communities began to deteriorate particularly after the introduction of the Sinhala Only Act in 1956 which sought to replace English and enshrine Sinhala as the only official language of the country, even though Tamil had also been in use for centuries. Tamils who had entered the public service in large numbers in the past, on the strength of their English education made possible by the missionary schools, now felt that in the future their children were going to be handicapped due to the language barrier imposed by the language act. Furthermore, it was also interpreted as a deliberate attempt to push the Tamils to a second-class status in the country, which they vehemently opposed, although albeit by peaceful and non-violent means. For instance, the leaders of the Federal Party (the main Tamil political party at the time) sat in on a *satyagraha*, a non-violent protest, on 5 June 1956 against the introduction of the Sinhala Only Bill in Parliament. They were assaulted by a crowd of Sinhala miscreants, and this was followed by further violent incidents against Tamils in Colombo. The ethnic problem escalated thereafter and began to dominate the politics of the country.

The war in Sri Lanka, which began in 1983, was brought to an end, at the close of 2001. The cessation of hostilities from December 2001, the lifting of the embargo in January 2002, the formalising of the ceasefire in February and the subsequent follow-up, have been the collective base for the current sustained rapprochement after two decades. There are many who see the recent developments in Sri Lanka as a possible model for peace making in a conflict-ridden region. This optimism notwithstanding, it will be premature to regard the Sri Lankan conflict as a closed chapter. The question still remains whether a stable, negotiated peace that entails mutual compromise and understanding on several long-pending issues, is ever possible in Sri Lanka. The stories of ethnic conflict and the civil war have been grim and arresting, all these years. There are still pending issues that provoke concern.

Ethnic Violence Against Tamils

The first ever major instance of ethnic violence against the Tamils in 1958 was put down fairly quickly by the government, but it could not prevent serious damage to the lives and property of Tamils in several parts of Sri Lanka. From then onwards, the ethnic problem took a new dimension. In the years up to 1950, there had been violence against various ethnic and religious groups in Sri Lanka. However the Sri Lanka Tamils, who formed around 11 per cent of the total population, were untouched, as they were considered to be 'sons of the soil'. But by the mid-1950s, the Sri Lanka Tamils came to be viewed as the 'traditional enemy' of the Sinhalese—an attitude which began among the petty bourgeoisie and was adopted by all classes by the 1980s.

After a relatively peaceful period, the situation began to deteriorate again in the 1970s. The introduction of language-wise standardisation of marks scored by students at the university entrance examination (the GCE Advanced Level examination) in the early 1970s adversely affected the admission of Tamil-language students to universities. Tamil youths aspiring to enter the universities after studying in the Tamil language found that they were discriminated against by the process of media-wise standardisation of marks. This angered them and the Tamils' accumulated grievances culminated in their demand for either a federal state or regional autonomy. The very concept of a federal state, however, was totally opposed by the governments in power, which the Tamils described as 'Sinhala governments'. The Sinhalese held a majority in Parliament, and under the parliamentary democratic system, decisions were arrived at on the basis of majority voting. The deteriorating ethnic relations and the accumulated grievances of the Tamils relating to language, education, employment, and land distribution, finally found expression in the demand for a separate state at the general elections in 1977. Immediately after the elections, violence broke out against the Tamils, beginning in the north and gradually spreading to the south of Sri Lanka. The demand for a separate state was not considered the cause of this ethnic violence unleashed against the Tamils, but it certainly provided a convenient excuse for racists to vent their anger (Sansoni Commission Report 1980). This was followed by the formation of militant Tamil groups and violent activities to establish a separate Tamil state called the 'Eelam'. What began as guerrilla warfare then turned into an open armed conflict between Tamil militants and government forces, which contributed further to the deterioration of relations between the two communities.

The killing of 13 Sinhala soldiers of the Sri Lankan army in northern Sri Lanka, in an ambush by the Liberation Tigers for Tamil Eelam (henceforth LTTE), the leading militant Tamil group, on 23 July 1983 resulted in the infamous ethnic riots against the Tamil community later that month. The country witnessed an unprecedented holocaust in which the Tamil community suffered enormous destruction and loss of life, besides large-scale destitution and homelessness. Riots continued to take place in 1977 and 1981, the latter confined mainly to the southern areas of Sri Lanka. The 1983 ethnic riots were by far the worst in terms of the scale and ferocity of the slaughter, arson and looting that took place. Irrespective of their age, sex or status, Tamils were pursued and killed in their homes, on the streets, in vehicles and even in hospitals and prisons.

A few months before the July riots, Indian Tamils, who had sought refuge in the Tamil areas of the north after the food shortages in 1973 and the riots of 1977, had been attacked by the army and driven back to the estates. This suggests that the attacks were well planned, long before widespread riots broke out that in July 1983. These riots effectively closed all avenues for an amicable settlement to the ethnic problem. In the meantime, moderate Tamil leaders were pushed aside, while the militants established themselves as the legitimate leaders of the Tamils. Consequently, the government was forced into a situation where, willingly or not, it had to negotiate with militant groups for a mutually acceptable solution to the problem.

In the meantime, the spillover effects of the prolonged ethnic conflict and the ongoing civil war had adverse consequences on estate Tamils, who were in no way party to the demand for a separate state by the Sri Lanka Tamils. The former became a target of attack by racists from other communities, particularly the majority Sinhalese, simply because of their Tamil identity. Furthermore, in the name of national security, estate Tamil youths were arrested by security forces on suspicion of having links with the northern Tamil militants and kept in custody for long periods of time without trial. In the context of the high security measures in operation, the fact that these youths did not possess National Identity Cards (NICs)[4] made them highly vulnerable to suspicion and arrest. Consequently, their movement outside the estate areas became restricted and they were unable to find jobs outside the estates in which they lived.

PART II: THE ESTATE TAMIL POPULATION

Historical Origin

The majority of the estate or plantation workers in Sri Lanka are Tamils of recent Indian origin, who can be traced to the 'coffee era' in Sri Lanka in the 19th century. Since the indigenous population (the Sinhala peasants) were not inclined to work as wage labourers on estates owned by British planters, the British were compelled to hire labourers from India. Coffee being a seasonal crop, the initial labour migration was in the form of free seasonal movement of workers between South India and Sri Lanka. When tea, a perennial crop, replaced coffee after the latter

was ravaged by plant disease, a permanent and resident labour force
was required. Large numbers of south Indian Tamils were brought in
the estates in specially constructed barrack-like 'line rooms', which led
to the emergence of a distinct Tamil community in the hilly areas of
Sri Lanka where the plantations were established. As a migrant community, the estate Tamils suffered the worst forms of exploitation, to
which similar communities elsewhere in the world were subjected.
They worked for abysmally low wages and were herded into intoler-
able, rectangular rooms, measuring 12 × 10 feet, and often with only
one entrance and no plumbing facilities. There were no toilets and
the water supply was usually from a common standpipe or a funnel
on the estate. The vast majority of Tamil workers continue to live in
these overcrowded, and dilapidated line rooms even today. A recent
survey revealed that there are 1,83,000 resident worker families in the
estates with a total population of 7,88,000. The available number of
housing units for this population is estimated at 1,78,000. Only 2 per
cent of this housing stock is in good condition, and a further 18 per
cent could be rehabilitated with minor repairs. At the other end of
the scale, 4 per cent of the stock is totally dilapidated and beyond
repair, while about 2 per cent requires such extensive repairs that
constructing new houses is thought to be less costly. Despite recent
efforts by the government to improve the Tamils' living conditions
through foreign donor-supported programmes, the situation is still
unsatisfactory.

Geographical Distribution of Estate Tamils

In 1971, out of the 12.7 million inhabitants of Sri Lanka, 1.16 million
lived and worked on estates, of whom approximately one million
was constituted by Indian Tamils who had migrated to Sri Lanka
since the mid-19th century, and their descendants. Today the Central
Province, where Satyodaya is located, has the largest concentration of Sri Lankan estate Tamils (46.5 per cent), while the provinces
of Uva and Sabaragamuwa hold 16.9 per cent and 15.9 per cent
respectively. Within the Central Province, the largest concentration is found in the Nuwara Eliya district, the heartland of the
tea plantations where estate Tamils account for 42.7 per cent of the
population.

Physical Separation and Segregation of Estate Tamils

Many of the estates were located in high altitude areas, far from traditional village settlements and isolated from the village communities. The estate workers' lives, like those of slaves, were carefully sealed off, not only from Sinhala villages in adjacent areas, but also from neighbouring estates. The labour policy followed by the planters emphasised this isolation. Outsiders were prevented from entering the estates by legal (and other) means, by the enactment of trespass laws. Furthermore, since estate labourers were clustered together in the middle of large estates, the workers developed a closed community life, continuing to follow their own culture and traditions (brought from their villages) without the benefits of any cultural cross-fertilisation. The estates had a separate social infrastructure, with a rudimentary health and education service for the workers' exclusive use. As these service centres were located in the heart of the estates, neighbouring villagers were prevented from reaching them easily and the opportunity to share them with the neighbouring communities was lost. This situation prevented any social contact between the estate workers and the villagers, who were already segregated by differences in language, religion and culture.

The separation of the plantation Tamils and rural Sinhala communities prevented them from understanding their mutual economic problems. The villagers were under the impression that the estate workers were economically better-off and secure, not realising that they also faced problems such as under-employment and unemployment, and low and fluctuating incomes. The estate workers, on the other hand, knew very little about the irregular income flows which the villagers suffered from, due to the vagaries of weather and the volatility of agricultural prices. Not having any economic, social or cultural exchanges with each other, and not sharing any social infrastructure facilities, the two communities existed side by side, but physically separated and socially segregated, each with its own economy, society and culture. Despite such separation and lack of mutual interaction, however, they co-existed peacefully for nearly 150 years without major conflicts. Furthermore, whenever a village existed in close proximity to an estate, there was some contact between the estate and village. In other words, left to themselves, estate worker and villager were quick to recognise an ally in each other and not a foe.

Deprivation of Citizenship Rights

A number of developments since Sri Lanka gained independence in 1948, disturbed this peaceful atmosphere. The first was denying the estate workers the right to citizenship, which had been contested by Sinhala leaders (who mainly belonged to the middle class) as early as the 1930s. When universal franchise was introduced in 1931 on the recommendation of the Donoughmore Commission, these Sinhala leaders successfully opposed the full and free extension of citizenship to the estate Tamils. This was further consolidated after independence by the Citizenship Act No. 18 of 1948 and the Parliamentary Elections (Amendment) Act of 1949. The 1949 Act stated that anyone who was not a citizen was not eligible to vote, thus simply negating their franchise. In 1949, the Indian Tamils were asked to seek citizenship rights under the Indian and Pakistani Residents (Citizenship) Act of 1949, but this Act had several provisions which made it difficult for them to obtain citizenship, even if they possessed all the necessary qualifications needed to register as Ceylon citizens. Estate workers, many of whom were illiterate, were not able to produce the complicated evidence demanded by the bureaucrats handling the case, and it is not surprising that nearly 84 per cent of those applying failed to secure registration under the Act. This left many of them without a nation: they were stateless, and suffered all the attendant consequences.

Land Reform and the Estate Tamils

The second development that had serious repercussions on the estate Tamils was the enactment of the Land Reform Laws in the 1970s and the critical food shortages of 1973, which caused the economic dislocation and displacement of large numbers of these workers. These land reform measures resulted in the nationalisation of foreign-owned plantations and those owned by nationals exceeding an area of 20 hectares. The latter category was located mostly in what is known as the mid-grown tea areas, where estates and Sinhala villages are situated in close proximity to each other. The post-reform institutional arrangements for managing the estate lands taken over by the state aimed to promote co-operative forms of agricultural production, and various co-operative organisations established for this purpose were handed over estate lands totalling approximately 107,650 hectares. These co-operative institutions functioned under a high degree of political control, pervading every aspect of their organisation and management, leading to confusion and misman-agement. Under the co-operative laws of the country, the Tamil workers resident on these estates were not eligible for membership of these co-operatives as they had been made non-citizens by the citizenship laws. Consequently, they were displaced from estate lands (and from their estate residence) and were substituted with Sinhala village labour. Large numbers of these displaced workers and their families were made homeless and became destitute, forced to roam neighbouring towns and villages as paupers, looking for food and employment. Some even drifted to Colombo, the capital city. It was these developments that made the Satyodaya Centre take up the cause of the plantation Tamils.

At the time of the takeover of estate lands under the First Land Reform Law (1972), it was generally argued that these lands should be returned to their legitimate owners, the Kandyan (Sinhala) peasantry. The Kandyan Sinhala leaders who represented these rural Sinhala peas-ants had always harboured a grievance against the opening of plantations on what they considered to be their traditional lands. It was claimed that the opening of plantations in these areas led to the dispossession of the Kandyan peasantry. Although, this 'dispossession' by plantations theory has been strongly contested by several researchers (de Silva, 1982), this view gained currency and came to be well established in the popular mind and the post-nationalisation developments gave expression to these views.

The land reform measure that was expected to bring significant benefits to the plantation workers thus turned into a nightmare for them. A violent campaign against Tamil estate workers was unleashed, which marked the beginning of ethnically motivated attacks on them. In some areas, the takeover was accomplished by expelling Tamil workers from estates on which they had lived and worked for generations, and the situation deteriorated to such an extent that serious concern was expressed both in Sri Lanka and abroad about the plight of the plantation workers. A documentary film on tea by the British television company Granada made the plight of the tea workers in Sri Lanka widely known in England. This was followed by protests by radical groups in England against the treatment of estate workers in Sri Lanka by prestigious companies such as Brooke Bond, as also a widespread campaign in Western countries urging people not to drink Sri Lankan tea produced from the sweat of the Indian Tamil workers.

PART III: SATYODAYA AND THE ESTATE TAMIL WORKERS

The Satyodaya Centre is a voluntary NGO registered with the Social Services Department of the Sri Lankan Government. It is an operational and advocacy NGO, which was established by the late Bishop Nanayakkara and Father Paul Caspersz. Both were believers in radical Christianity and were deeply committed to social justice and equality, feeling that religion, and Christianity in particular, should be a stimulating force for social change and challenge political institutions to ensure that they function for the benefit of all and liberate the oppressed. This shared conviction led to their setting up the Satyodaya Centre on 11 February 1972. Although the Centre was established by two priests, it can by no means be called a religious organisation, and in 1974 they initiated a Marxist-Christian dialogue, the first such dialogue to be held in Asia. Its founders claimed that the Centre was established as an attempt to discover the potential for desirable social change in all religions; and recognising that Sri Lanka is a multi-ethnic country, the Centre views religion as an element of secular society. It was this premise that shaped the development of the Centre in its early years. Having started with just two members, it has grown today into a mixed community of inter-ethnic, inter-religious, inter-linguistic, inter-generational and inter-social groups which live and work together. According to Elizabeth O' Keele of the Jesuit Refugee Service Centre (1994) 'this proactive community is particularly striking in a country where nearly 40,000 of its 18 million people have been killed in the 17 year old civil war drawn on ethnic lines'.[5]

Satyodaya's Objectives

Through its Social Research and Encounter programmes, Satyodaya maintains contact with deprived groups and marginal communities. Its mission, as its name implies, is one of thought and action, achieved through research, writing pitched at high, middle, and popular levels, organising and conducting seminars and conferences, and experimenting in socialist groups living together at the Centre and implementing projects. The Centre was from the start a joint effort to work towards a just society—a commitment reflected in its objectives:

1. To strive to promote social justice.
2. To strive to promote cultural, economic, civil and social activities among people living in villages, estates, and town areas.
3. To strive for unity and mutual understanding and to eliminate disunity and misunderstanding among different communities, in the belief that Sri Lanka is and should continue to be a plural society.
4. To strive to eradicate unjust divisions among the people.

The aims and objectives of Satyodaya can thus be broadly summarised as the pursuit of peace with justice; the promotion of cultural, social and civic activities of people in the areas in which it works; and the promotion of inter-ethnic justice in the plural society of Sri Lanka.

The Centre started with the vision of religion interacting with society, but was later increasingly drawn towards social action. It became an inter-ethnic and inter-religious community whose objective was to release people from the structures of injustice and oppression through a radical understanding of religion and the ideology of an equalitarian society. A combination of events and circumstances later drew its attention to the field of inter-communal peace.

From the winter of 1972, following the start of the nationalisation of estates, Satyodaya was also drawn into an examination of plantation-area issues. During the early 1970s, plantations in Sri Lanka went through a difficult period. A lecture delivered at the Satyodaya Centre by Hector Abhayavardena, a veteran Marxist intellectual, on 'The Situation of the Plantation Workers' highlighted the dangers of the developments in the plantation areas and took up the cause of the estate (or plantation) Tamil workers, who were the most disadvantaged community in the country in terms of income, wealth, education, health, and housing. Sri Lanka had achieved a high quality of life as measured by the Human Development Index (HDI)[6] which was comparable to that of some developed countries. In contrast to this overall achievement, the plantation Tamil community continues to be socially and educationally backward. For historical and other reasons, many of the welfare services provided by the state fail to reach the Tamils, while lack of access to various infrastructure facilities and services handicaps their social advancement. The deprivation of citizenship rights after independence, and their consequent, non-representation in Parliament and other local government institutions, hindered their participation as equal citizens in the development process which took place in the country for almost four decades, until their citizenship rights were restored in 1988.

The ethnic problem further added to their misery, for despite belonging to a distinct Sri Lanka Tamil community and despite not demanding a separate state, in a situation of bitter ethnic conflict they are a target for attack by racists from other communities, particularly the majority Sinhalese, simply because they are Tamils. Communal attacks on the plantation community have become frequent since the takeover of estates. Satyodaya, which stands for justice and equality among different ethnic groups and communal harmony and peace in the country, therefore began to concentrate on the plantation areas.

The Evolution of Satyodaya

From its inception in 1972 up to 1998, Satyodaya went through a number of changes. Its evolution can be analysed in terms of Korten's theory of the linear evolution of NGOs. According to Korten (1987), NGOs tend to grow through a linear evolutionary development process, either individually or collectively, and reach a 'third generation stage'. From being involved in relief and welfare activities (first generation), many NGOs move on to addressing the structural context of self-help action through organisation and mobilisation of local resources (second generation). In their final stage, they seek to change institutions and policies, at national as well as sub-national levels, that inhibit effective self-help action.

Three stages of development in the evolution of Satyodaya have been identified by Samarajeewa and Palaniappan (1993). At first, its work centred on research and relief activities, where working *for* the people was the rule of the day. But later, it switched to working *with* the people, where community participation was encouraged. Today empowering people has become the focus of its work. On the basis of this evolutionary process, the history of Satyodaya can be divided into three periods for easy analysis:

1972–83:   Academic research seems to have been the prime concern of Satyodaya during its early years. However, the impact of land reform (from 1972 to 1975) on the plantation workers, the near-famine that struck the lower strata of society in the plantation areas during the 1973–75 period, and the successive waves of communal riots that hit these workers after 1977 compelled Satyodaya to involve itself in increased field-level activities, especially in the affected areas. Satyodaya assisted those who were in need and carried out a number of welfare programmes; thus relief and rehabilitation work absorbed much of its attention during this period. It functioned as a charity, supplying hand-outs of milk and food to the malnourished and providing emergency relief (clothing and dry rations) to victims of ethnic violence. Its field activities during these years chiefly took the following forms:

1. Frequent contacts with estate workers and peasants in their homes and workplaces in order to gain an understanding of their situation.

2. The creation of simple community centres in its workplaces where people could meet to read newspapers, play indoor and outdoor games, organise pre-school or sewing classes or small production units, and above all strengthen a sense of community feeling. The development of such a community spirit was of great importance in the context of the inter-community tension prevailing in the country.

3. The organisation of health programmes, through educational and mobile clinics, to care for simple wounds and ordinary ailments, and assisting more difficult cases to contact regular hospital services.

4. The organisation of seminar programmes, the most formal of which were the weekend bilingual Leadership Seminars held at the Satyodaya Centre for a mixed group of Sinhala village and estate Tamil youth. In addition, scores of informal seminars were held out in the field, on the estates, and in the villages.

5. Working with Indian repatriates and repatriates to-be; this included educational work and assistance of various kinds to the repatriates.

1984–89:   In its second phase, starting from 1984, Satyodaya experienced a change. Its field activities were strengthened by the introduction of changes in its organisational structure. Field activities went beyond addressing the immediate needs of the people and their focus shifted to tackling the root causes of the problems faced, with a view to finding lasting solutions. Constant communication was maintained with the people; community centres were established as a base for initiating activities and for mobilising people to participate in activities organised by them. In other words, the concept of working with the people emerged during this phase.

Satyodaya began to work with poor and marginalised groups in society but did not confine itself to charity only. Stemming from its commitment to social justice and peace, it began to concentrate on bringing the Sinhala villager and the Tamil estate worker to its community centres and libraries. Here they were given an opportunity to meet each other and to begin to remove the stereotyped images that the media and the political milieu had created.

Post-1990:   From 1990 onwards, a new outlook was experienced in almost every aspect of Satyodaya's community development activities. It attempted to work as a People's Organisation (PO), defined as an entity which has a common vision and set of goals that are shared with the communities it works with. The concept of empowering people became its focus, and this empowering exercise was expected to be a gradual process with an integrated approach involving the following five phases:

1. The development of a close relationship with the target population and being accepted by it.
2. The study of the basic socio-economic background of the community.
3. The identification of potential community leaders and strengthening them with necessary leadership and organisational skills and attitudes.
4. The mobilisation of the target group with the help of their identified and trained leaders, so that collective activities designed to answer to their needs could be carried out.
5. The empowerment of the people.

In keeping with these five phases, Satyodaya introduced a systematic approach to the planning and implementation of its programmes, as well as the decentralisation of management, and the co-ordination of field work. Thus, while Phase one was described as working *for* the people and Phase two as working *with* the people, in Phase three Satyodaya expects people to work *with* it. It considers this to be not an ideal, but a consciously pursued goal. In other words, Satyodaya switched from pure academic research to social action for inter-communal peace and justice from 1977–89, and then shifted towards evolving into a People's Organisation[7] or movement in the post-1990 period.

Re-organisation of Satyodaya

During the organisation's first 25 years, its founder co-ordinator was responsible for practically all its activities. However, from being a small organisation consisting of only a few members, Satyodaya has grown into a multi-faceted organisation with around 50 full-time members over the years. With the addition of new workplaces and work programmes, its field work also grew (in its range and the number of programmes implemented). Much of this work was carried out without any written rules and regulations. For instance, no letters of appointment had been issued to anyone who worked with Satyodaya, nor was there any formal allocation of work to each member or supervision of the work carried out by them. As a result, everyone did everything, and work was based on the trust and confidence placed on Satyodaya's leader, who was felt to be totally committed to fulfilling the objectives of the organisation. However, there is no doubt that Satyodaya had grown in an unsystematic and unplanned manner. As the number of volunteers increased, administrative problems began to manifest themselves; and a complete re-structuring became inevitable in order to introduce some order in the payment of remunerations, and to allocate clearly and systematically the work expected of each person in the organisation. The retirement of Fr. Caspersz as co-ordinator provided the right opportunity for such a restructuring. After several discussions, the entire Satyodaya community agreed to tender its resignation and re-apply for membership. This was carried out through a consensus about the modus operandi of the restructuring process, and at the beginning of 1996 the Co-ordinator began transferring the entire responsibility of running Satyodaya to the new leadership. This process was successfully completed by the end of December 1996.

Restructuring and Collective Leadership

With the retirement of the Founder-Co-ordinator and the restructuring of Satyodaya, six units—each with its own head and a collective leadership—were set up. These Heads of Units were entrusted with the responsibility for the smooth functioning of their respective units. This collective leadership is exercised through the Executive Committee (EXCO), comprising 11 members, who include the six Unit Heads of the Satyodaya Centre. The six units are Field Programmes; Administration; Finance; Library and Research; Maintenance and Improvement of Infrastructure; and Farm and Agricultural Training. Every effort was made to ensure that the EXCO is inter-ethnic, inter-linguistic, inter-religious, and inter-sex in its composition. At the end of 1996, for instance, the EXCO had seven Sinhalese, three Tamils and one Burgher, of whom seven were Buddhist, three Hindu and one Christian. Four were women and seven were men (Satyodaya Annual Report, 1996/97). The EXCO elects five principal office-bearers—Chairperson, Secretary, Treasurer, Assistant Chairperson, and Assistant Secretary—who form the core of the collective leadership.

The decision-making process is now allied to the delegation of duties and responsibilities, and everyone within the respective unit participates in the decision-making process. This new system has further strengthened the process of participatory democracy and decentralisation of the affairs of the organisation, and calls for a greater sense of responsibility from each one of its members.

Satyodaya's Field Activities

Satyodaya's field work is generally designed to meet its three main emphases: to strengthen civil society, and to address the problem of environment and the position of women in society. Its specific field activities include community organisation, to help people find solutions to their problems through collective effort, by organising and co-ordinating income-generating projects, self-employment schemes and vocational training programmes, establishing reading rooms/clubs, organising health and nutrition programmes and food-for-work (*shramadana*) programmes. A number of field programmes are therefore organised under its Field Operations Unit, carried out at two levels:

i) **Base-Level Programmes:**   At the base level (village or estate level), community organisation and development programmes are conducted by People's Societies in collaboration with Satyodaya. These usually involve the construction of community centres and reading rooms, housing, renovation of old school buildings, and include organising savings and credit schemes.

Community centres have been established in almost all the locations where Satyodaya works. The particular mix of functions and projects carried out at the different centres by the People's Societies that have been created depends on the needs of the locality. In one centre house construction might be organised, while somewhere else the Centre may concentrate on building and maintaining a safe water supply system to a village or running a vocational training programme. The ideology behind these activities is to build self-sustaining, democratic and accountable organisations for local development, with informed individuals providing constructive criticism and leadership. Therefore, in each Centre there is a reading room where current newspapers, periodicals and books are kept together with various 'how to' manuals. Meetings to discuss local and more general problems are convened in these reading rooms, and the Satyodaya Centre provides training in book-keeping, legal and technical services, and also assists in obtaining credit. Through these activities, it tries to unite groups of citizens for local development work and to foster co-operation and understanding among them.

Some of the community centres established by People's Societies are better organised than others, but in terms of the solidarity of their members, participation in the work programmes, the nature of the discussions and meetings that take place, decision-making processes, dealings with financial matters, maintenance of records and minutes and initiating programmes, nearly two-thirds of the centres are in a healthy condition. Berawila, a remote village surrounded by mountains with very difficult access roads and footpaths, is cut off from the nearest town by nearly 23 km. Satyodaya has worked in this village since 1985 and villagers have been mobilised on the basis of their felt needs, such as access to clean drinking water. Due to the lack of proper roads, the villagers used to walk long distances to buy their daily provisions. So in January 1993 a co-operative sales centre was started in the village on Satyodaya's initiative, and seven members raised a loan of Rs 40,000 from Satyodaya's Income-Generating Programme. Over time, membership of the sales centre has grown and part of the loan has been repaid, the daily turnover of the centre being around Rs 2,000. All profits are channelled into the People's Society, to be used for small development programmes in the village. A pre-school is run by the Centre, and about 40 children attend the school with two teachers. Children, plus expectant and lactating mothers, are given a balanced mid-day meal every day, for which half the cost is met by Satyodaya and the other half by the parents.

The Centre has also constructed a number of drinking-water wells, shared with people in a nearby estate, which provides an opportunity for Sinhala and Tamil youths to meet each other. Satyodaya runs a number of supporting programmes in the village, such as *shramadana*, home gardening, pre-school, nutrition, income-generation and women's programmes in the village. These have provided a new experience in community work for Satyodaya and have proved to be replicable. In all workplaces, according to the needs identified by the people, common wells or wooden bridges have been built, or existing ones repaired, and attention is also paid to environmental sanitation, health and nutrition.

ii) **General Area Programmes:**   These include the following educational and awareness programmes:

- Leadership training/pre-school/economic activities/public seminars
- Audio-visual programmes
- Relief and rehabilitation programme
- Vocational training programme

Besides these, Satyodaya also runs two special programmes for nutrition (including an agricultural training programme) and women's issues.

Field programmes are carried out in several locations. A total of 70 programmes are run in all five different geographical areas—44 on estates, 19 in villages and seven in urban settlements. Satyodaya's work is heavily concentrated on the estate sector as Satyodaya believes that the dominant or national-level development programmes do not reach the real poor and, therefore, Satyodaya field programmes should cater to those who fail to benefit from such programmes. In some estates

Satyodaya has undertaken housing schemes with the participation of resident families.

Graigingilt Estate Housing Scheme

Graigingilt is an abandoned tea estate with 72 resident Tamil families who were badly affected by the ethnic riots of 1977. In the immediate aftermath of the riots, Satyodaya began implementing a relief and rehabilitation programme on the estate. After a few weeks this was stopped, with only the pre-school programme continuing in a small community centre. Later, Satyodaya began a full-scale programme of community organisation which included the pre-school programme already in progress, a health and nutrition programme, food-for-work programmes and training for self-employment.

The resident families on the estate had hitherto been living in single line-rooms of 10 × 12 feet which were dilapidated, unhygienic and totally unfit for human occupation. Early in 1992, the Helvetas—a Swiss donor-partner of Satyodaya—announced that the Swiss Association of House Owners was willing to sponsor a housing project for the poor. Satyodaya seized this opportunity to embark on a housing scheme on the Graigingilt estate. Ten acres of land were purchased for this purpose with the personal savings of the resident families under the Janasaviya programme (a poverty-alleviation programme implemented by the government, under which part of the money given to the poor was saved in their name), a loan from Satyodaya, and some funding from the NOVIB (a Dutch donor organisation). The land was blocked into 80 lots, each consisting of 16 perches (1/16th of an acre). Satyodaya Rural Technical Services assisted with the technical aspects of the infrastructure, especially for water supply and drainage. Insufficient water had been a major problem on the estate, so Satyodaya organised a number of *shramadana* programmes to clean and repair existing and badly damaged canals, and water supply was restored to the estate. Estate residents actively participated in these activities, which also provided an opportunity to raise their level of awareness.

By the end of 1999, 70 houses had been completed and only one family had no new home as there was some problem with the land allocated to them. Each family paid Rs 200 per month to refund the loan given by Satyodaya, in addition to the lump sum some families had paid out of their Janasaviya savings. It is expected that each family will pay about Rs 50,000 as its contribution to the cost of the house and the land. In constructing their houses each family proceeds at its own pace.

Women's Programme

The women's programme plays an important role in Satyodaya's community development activities. The main objective of this programme is to involve women fully in the community development process and thereby enable women to take their due place in society. The following agenda was designed to enhance women's participation in Satyodaya's development programmes in the villages and on the estates:

- The strengthening of women's institutions;
- The assertion of women's rights to participate in decision-making;
- The creation of women's awareness programmes for social, economic, and political problems;
- The promotion of ethnic understanding among women;
- The creation of activities to help estate women overcome the monotony of their life;

A committee consisting of 30 women was organised, with five women from each area where Satyodaya works. These women leaders were helped to understand women's problems, the causes for these problems, and steps to be taken to find solutions to them. These women, in turn, organised women's committees in their own areas to train women and to carry out work programmes for the development of women. Studies carried out by Satyodaya on women and children have identified the following common problems for women in these areas: a low level of education, health-related problems, malnutrition, a lack of understanding of their problems and a lack of time and opportunity to improve their lot.

Satyodaya conducted women-focused adult education and health education programmes in several of its workplaces. Subjects such as women's issues, male domination, and gender awareness were discussed, and small-scale income-generating activities such as animal husbandry, sewing, home gardening and commercialised flower growing were taught. Many of the women who completed this training are now actively involved in these activities.

Carrying out the Field Programmes

Through experience, Satyodaya has found that many of the problems faced can only be solved through promoting and strengthening People's Societies—that is, by strengthening civil society. 'Problems' can be at the individual level, community level, or at the national level, and different solutions to each need to be found. At the individual level, there exists a problem of survival, the meeting of the most basic needs. At the community level, these basic needs are reflected collectively in the community, such as water supply, sanitation, education, land, and housing, and in recent times in Sri Lanka, communal harmony and security can also be classified as basic needs. Satyodaya felt that the poor need to be organised to seek solutions to these problems through collective action. Therefore, its approach has been to promote People's Societies at each of its workplaces. The office-bearers of these societies, who are elected members by their peers, form an area committee; and the Field Programme Co-ordinator or the Area Co-ordinator of Satyodaya for the respective area functions as Chairperson of the committee. For instance, if there are five office-bearers in each People's Society, and there are 10 Societies in a given area, then the area committee will consist of 50 members. They meet once every three months to plan their activities, and the committee is expected to prepare a programme for the entire area which tackles common problems prevailing in the area.

Satyodaya does not commit itself to support all the activities planned by these committees. However, it usually carries out a pilot project for the community in order to build its confidence, and then asks the area committee to pressurise the relevant state authorities to supply the resources and services provided previously by Satyodaya. The committee provides a place for people to meet and discuss the problems of their own locality and to share their views on Sri Lanka's current problems. The area committees are expected to provide everything needed for the empowerment of the poor, and offer ordinary people a chance to act on matters outside their own constituency.

Satyodaya's goal has always been to transfer power to the people. It constantly asks itself how long it should work in a given estate, village or urban area. It has always been problematic to withdraw from a workplace for practical reasons, so the Centre eventually decided to work on a five-year plan before withdrawing, conscious that some areas may need less time and others, more.

Satyodaya strengthens the People's Societies it has helped to create at its workplaces by imparting organisational skills and financial stability through various programmes which expose the People's Societies to various outside institutions. After the five-year period, these workplaces are expected to work closely with their respective area committees so the beneficiaries themselves take the lead in all stages of field work, from planning to evaluation. In this respect, the area committee plays a vital role, and is expected to ensure the maximum participation of people in the area.

Planning, Implementation and Monitoring of Field Work

The conscious goal of this exercise has been to pass on power to the people or to empower them in a gradual manner. This takes place at two levels:

i) **In the Field:**   Through their area committee, people in the area are encouraged to take the lead in all stages of field work from planning to evaluation. This calls for a high degree of perception and a sense of responsibility, and from our discussions with people, it was found that when they know they are truly in charge of planning and implementing programmes for their own advancement, they quickly acquire the skills necessary for such analysis and begin to show a considerable seriousness of purpose.

ii) **At Satyodaya:**   Once a month on Friday, a Field Staff meeting is held at the Satyodaya Centre in which the Deputy Co-ordinator of the Centre and the Programme Co-ordinators also participate. A file is maintained to record matters discussed and, according to available records, some important aspects of field work discussed at these meetings include:

- programme designing, planning and other activities of the programme cycle;
- presentation of feasibility reports and programme planning;
- presentation of monthly planning and monthly reports;

- policy on women's issues and preparation of women's programmes;
- the importance of pre-school;
- characteristics of People's Societies and their financial sustainability;
- survey techniques, data collection, and preparation of questionnaires;
- assessing malnutrition.

The items discussed confirm that the Friday meetings are held not only to discuss field programmes and monitoring of these programmes, but also to give the staff some training in various tasks related to field work.

Every six months, the Monitoring Unit prepares a report which helps the EXCO to assess the progress of projects and to take steps, where necessary, to speed up any activities whose progress is found to be slow or below expectation. Formal and informal meetings of small groups are also held from time to time to discuss the successes and failures of the field programmes. As time passes, Satyodaya members gradually withdraw into the background allowing the People's Societies to carry out the programmes on their own. Satyodaya only extends its support when requested by the local societies.

The People's Societies are expected to be mindful of the following eight points in their work:

1. The formation and functioning of a well-organised society.
2. That active office-bearers are motivated by a spirit of leadership through service to the community, their motto being, 'We are here not to be served but to serve'.
3. The maintenance of a record of active members.
4. The maintenance of a record of the payment of membership fees.
5. The systematic recording of attendance at general meetings and the maintenance of proper minutes of proceedings of meetings.
6. The systematic recording of attendance at monthly committee meetings of office-bearers and of minutes of proceedings.
7. A constitution for each local society.

8. The opening of a bank account for the Society and the maintenance of a cash book.

It was found that working within these guidelines has helped the People's Societies to improve their level of performance.

Satyodaya's Networking Strategy

Satyodaya has been attempting to build a society based on justice and peace and started working at different levels towards this end. At the grassroots level it works in the villages, on the estates, and in urban areas directly with the people. At provincial and national levels it collaborates with others to deal with social problems and matters connected with state policies. For instance, it initiated the Co-ordinating Secretariat for Plantation Areas (CSPA) in 1974 in order to engage in common action with several like-minded organisations and with trade unions in the plantation sector, to deal with problems created by the nationalisation of estates (as has already been explained). In 1979, it initiated the Movement for Inter-Racial Justice and Equality (MIRJE) to deal with the worsening ethnic problem in the country. At the regional level, it is an active member of the People's Plan for the 21st Century Movement (PP 21), and at the international level, it works in solidarity with like-minded individuals and organisations to promote a just world order.

Satyodaya as a Unique NGO

Recently Satyodaya has been trying to evolve into a People's Organisation (PO), but has faced some difficulties in doing so. For an organisation to be a PO, people should be able to participate in decision-making processes at all levels within the organisation. Satyodaya has therefore established People's Societies at its workplaces and area committees, consisting of representatives of these Societies at the area level in order to ensure people's participation in planning, implementing and evaluating projects, and programmes for their own development. Area committees are represented in the Satyodaya apex decision-making body–the EXCO–but the Area Co-ordinators who represent these area committees happen to be Satyodaya employees. Thus, people's participation at the top level of the decision-making process is found to be wanting. Satyodaya has therefore yet to evolve into a real PO. However, it can undoubtedly be described as special among NGOs in Sri Lanka. Though many of its activities are not different from those of other NGOs, some are certainly unique:

1. In the early 1970s it took the initiative to form the CSPA as an umbrella organisation for the NGOs working in the plantation areas to co-ordinate their activities.

2. As Satyodaya's aim is to promote inter-ethnic justice and peace in the plural society of Sri Lanka, it initiated action to create the MIRJE in 1979, and the Co-ordinator of Satyodaya himself served as the National Co-ordinator of the MIRJE in its early stages. Just as the problems created by the nationalisation of estate lands induced the Satyodaya to take the initiative to set up the CSPA in 1974, the ethnic riots of 1977 played a key role in inspiring it to initiate action on forming the MIRJE. During the riots, the father of one of the resident members of Satyodaya was cruelly burnt to death in a shop set on fire by miscreants, while his house was ransacked in a nearby town around the same time. This urged the Satyodaya to set up the MIRJE, and later the victim's son became an activist in the MIRJE to promote peace and understanding among the different ethnic communities in the country.

3. The initiative taken by Satyodaya in organising the daily-paid labourers and the small pavement hawkers in the Kandy market can be considered another unique service. Daily-paid workers, or *nattamis*, have a very low status in society. They are considered to belong to a lower caste by the dominant culture and are often labelled as thugs, pickpockets and thieves. On the initiative taken by Satyodaya, they formed themselves into an association which, has helped them to bargain with their employers—the wholesale vegetable dealers—for better wages. This association has organised a *Maranadara* society (a funeral-donation society) to help its members in times of family bereavement. The association maintains a bank account and extends small loans to its members in times of distress. After the formation of the association, these *nattamis* claim that they have been able to gain some recognition in their place

of work and in society, and that their relationship with their
employers, in particular, has improved.

4. Satyodaya also helped small pavement hawkers in the Kandy
central market to form the Small Pavement Hawkers' Association. Until this association was formed, these hawkers had
no legal authority to sell goods (mainly vegetables) within
or in the vicinity of the market complex. As a result, they
were constantly harassed by the police and the munici-
pal officials. After forming the Association, they have been
able to act collectively and secure permission to sell their
goods in and around the market. Each hawker now pays
Rs 10 per day as rent to the municipality and, since an
official receipt is issued for it, they have gained legal recognition and are no longer harassed. The Association also
provides several benefits to its members: it maintains a
fund to extend distress loans and also organises sports activities, religious festivities, and food-for-work programmes
among them. More importantly, it has extended assistance
to victims of ethnic violence and supplied medicine, as a
national service, to soldiers injured in the ongoing civil
war.

Organising the daily-paid workers and the small pavement hawkers can
be considered a unique service rendered by Satyodaya, and the benefits
cannot be measured only in quantitative terms.

Part IV: Satyodaya's Experience with Empowerment Efforts

The estate Tamils and the Sinhala peasants with whom Satyodaya
works are locked in poverty and enslaved by structures that perpetuate
dependency and oppression. Satyodaya tried to help them to liberate
themselves from their situation through a process of empowerment.
Empowerment refers to the ability of people to organise and influence
change on the basis of their access to knowledge, to political processes,
and to financial, social, and natural resources. Such empowerment cannot be created by outside agents such as NGOs, but it can certainly raise
their consciousness. The poor, the marginalised, and the excluded are
responsible for their own empowerment. Consciousness-raising is the

first indispensable step towards enhancing people's empowerment (or people power), which Satyodaya tries to achieve through its awareness programmes and development work. Initially, Satyodaya worked *for* the people by organising relief and rehabilitation for victims of man-made and natural disasters. In 1977, for instance, it directly helped 2,663 estate-worker families who had lost everything but their lives due to that year's ethnic riots. Similarly, it helped some estate worker families who were affected by severe drought conditions in 1981. It also helped the poor and the malnourished by supplying them with food, and the sick by providing basic drugs and helping them to reach the nearest hospitals for further treatment. In the second stage, it worked *with* the people, the main objective being to raise their level of awareness. It organised seminars and workshops to create awareness about their problems and the causes for it. Currently, it is engaged in facilitating the empowerment of people through organising People's Societies and area committees so that they can plan and implement programmes for their own development. Development work is a tool for empowerment: it recognises the fact that people have the capacity to organise them-selves, and to decide on their own the appropriate methods and kind of development best suited for their needs. Satyodaya has tried to enhance this capacity and to ensure full participation of the people in bringing about genuine social change. For this purpose, it provides a number of supporting services such as leadership training, vocational training, awareness creation, self-employment, and programmes to enhance the skills and capacities of women, the main focus group of its activities being the youth. It expects to withdraw from active involvement in its workplaces after five years, but it has faced difficulties in doing so.

Satyodaya has succeeded in raising awareness among the poor in the villages and estates where it works. But its task of empowering people through its awareness programmes and supporting services has been a difficult one in the case of the plantation workers, for the following reasons:

1. As captive labour, plantation workers are totally dependent on the estate management for the provision of their needs. This almost fatalistic dependency syndrome, a legacy of several generations of semi-slavery on the estates, which still per-sists among them, acts as a major barrier to their own social and economic advancement. Their emancipation from this

captive-labour mentality is a prerequisite for their empowerment, but this requires fundamental changes in the system of organisation and management of the plantations. Satyodaya, through its research, publications, and seminars, has tried to make various sections of the community aware of the need for change in the system of organisation and management of the estates.

2. The current ethnic problem, the civil war, and the consequent security situation in Sri Lanka also hampers the work of NGOs among plantation workers. Satyodaya, in fact, had to work in a hostile environment. Any outside organisation attempting to establish operations among the plantation workers is suspect in the eyes of the management and security forces. Furthermore, NGOs cannot enter estates without prior permission from the management, and such permission is not always easy to obtain.

3. The estate workers' statelessness, their treatment as second-class citizens, and a lack of political patronage, also act against their empowerment, so that it tends to be slower when compared to that of the rural peasants.

Satyodaya and Inter-Ethnic Peace and Harmony

In its attempts to bring about peace and harmony between plantation workers and the Sinhala villagers in the plantation areas, Satyodaya organised various programmes in the villages, on the estates, and at the Satyodaya Centre itself, where youths belonging to the two communities were brought together. These programmes, seminars, and workshops are nearly always bilingual, with a deliberate mixing of ethnic participants so that at the end of the seminar they leave not only having learnt something about the subject on which training was given, but having learnt how to live with members of other communities. In residential programmes, Sinhala and Tamil participants are made to share rooms, which was a new experience for many of them. Initially, the estate youths were reluctant to do so, but as time went on they overcame their unease, were able to build up their self-confidence, and began to actively participate in these programmes. In this sense, Satyodaya's efforts certainly have had some positive effects on the youth. It was also found that in areas where Satyodaya worked, inter-ethnic understanding has been healthier than elsewhere (for instance, during outbreaks of ethnic violence there was less or no violence in these areas).

Inter-Ethnic Relations at the National Level

Satyodaya worked closely with the MIRJE for many years in an attempt to find immediate, short-term, and long-term solutions to the ethnic problem. However, this has been a difficult task. After working in the field for several years, with a sense of sadness and impotence, it had to settle for a long-term solution to the problem. Due to the lack of moral and political will to hammer out a peaceful solution by the protagonists on both sides of the ethnic divide, the problem continues to haunt the country and is in the grip of a costly civil war in terms of human lives and finances. Nevertheless, Satyodaya continues to work with faith and hope for what it calls 'inter-ethnic peace founded upon justice'.

PART V: LESSONS FROM SATYODAYA

Establishing Links with Like-Minded Organisations

Satyodaya started out with very broad objectives but, with Sri Lanka's changing circumstances, its focus turned towards two particular problems: building inter-ethnic harmony and peace in a situation of bitter ethnic conflict and the outbreak of ethnically-oriented violence; and organising relief and rehabilitation for the estate Tamil workers affected by the nationalisation of estate lands, while also working for inter-ethnic harmony in the plantation areas, particularly after the ethnic riots of 1977.

As a relatively small organisation, Satyodaya could not have accomplished much by itself, considering the complicated nature of the problems it attempted to tackle. But by establishing links with other like-minded organisations and by initiating the creation of new affiliates, it was able to work on a wider front. It played a crucial role in setting up the CSPA to co-ordinate the activities of a number of NGOs working in the plantation areas. Similarly, it initiated the establishment of the MIRJE to deal with the ethnic problem. The co-ordinator of Satyodaya himself was also the co-ordinator of these two organisations in their early stages. Both organisations were very active in the field during the critical period of the 1970s and 1980s. This demonstrates how much a small organisation, by linking up with other like-minded organisations, can do.

Working in an Environment of Ethnic Conflict

Satyodaya's main concern was the welfare of estate Tamil workers, but its programmes in the field and at the Satyodaya Centre were extended to the Sinhala villagers living in the plantation areas as well. This was felt necessary because of the prevailing ethnic problem in the country, the statelessness of the estate Tamils, and the Kandyan Sinhala attitude towards the estate Tamil community. Since one of Satyodaya's objectives is inter-ethnic harmony and peace, it had to work with both communities in order to bring about mutual understanding and acceptance between them. Furthermore, working with the estate Tamil community alone may have created jealousy among the Sinhala peasants, who are equally poor and deprived. It is also likely that the politicians from the area may have created obstacles to its activities on the grounds that it was working only for the estate Tamils while the Sinhala villagers also deserve similar assistance. Satyodaya acted wisely by including the Sinhala peasants in its programmes, which shows that if any NGO working among disadvantaged groups is to succeed, it cannot ignore the general social and political environment in which it works.

Satyodaya's Evolutionary Process

Satyodaya's evolution from a research-based organisation to a social action-oriented one that is attempting to evolve into a People's Organisation is noteworthy. While still engaged in relief and welfare activities, it now concentrates on the empowerment of the people with whom it works by introducing participatory methods in all its activities. Through setting up People's Societies in its workplaces and area committees in the wider geographical areas in which these workplaces are located, it was able to play a catalytic role in the empowerment process at the grassroots level. The beneficiaries of Satyodaya programmes, however, continue to look at it as a relief organisation and expect material benefits from it. As a result, it has found it difficult to withdraw from its workplaces so as to make people themselves responsible for their advancement. Withdrawal has been a difficult problem to many NGOs working in the field. Nevertheless, Satyodaya has succeeded in initiating the process of transferring power to the people.

The Transfer of Power within NGOs

For 25 years since its inception, Satyodaya had worked as a loosely structured organisation with minimum rules and regulations and no written constitution. Its Founder-Co-ordinator remained the organisation's livewire. With the gradual expansion of the organisation in terms of the number of people working for it, the number of work places, the number of geographical areas covered, and the number of field activities, it became necessary to have a set of rules and regulations, especially with the impending retirement of the Co-ordinator. A collective leadership was established and some organisational re-structuring introduced to substitute for the loss of the dynamic leadership provided by the Founder-Co-ordinator. And during the short period of its existence, this collective leadership seems to have worked well.

The dynamic leadership of a single individual has been the key to the success of many NGOs, and it has been the experience of several of these NGOs that the retirement or death of such a leader not only created a vacuum but also led to their collapse. Satyodaya overcame this problem by re-structuring and transferring of power to a collective leadership. This can be a useful lesson to other organisations in similar situations.

CONCLUSION

The primary objective of Satyodaya as a people-oriented organisation was to participate in the struggle of the poor and the oppressed for liberation, self-reliance and the achievement of a better quality of life. The estate Tamils and the Sinhala peasants with whom it works are locked in poverty and enslaved by structures that exploit and perpetuate dependency and oppression among them. Satyodaya, in its small way, tried to help them to free themselves of these structures. It realised that the first step towards this was consciousness-raising, which would result in their empowerment. It therefore conducted various consciousness-raising seminars and workshops, and used its development work as a tool for empowerment, recognising that people have the capacity to organise themselves and make their own decisions about the appropriate development methods suited to their needs. But Satyodaya had to work in an environment of ethnic conflict and open ethnic violence, and also suffered other constraints, such as restrictions by estate management; lack of political support; people's attitudes; communication barriers due to the illiteracy of its constituency, and lack of time and interest on their part; lack of infrastructure in the areas where it works; and cultural barriers against women NGO workers.

Despite these constraints, Satyodaya has been able to create social and political awareness among a small group of people who are expected to carry this message to wider sections of the community.

NOTES

1. Estate workers have always been close to my heart, as I, too, belong to the Indian Tamil community in Sri Lanka, of which the estate workers form a part.
2. In fact the northern tip of the Jaffna peninsula, the northernmost point of Sri Lanka, is closer to India than to the capital city of Colombo.
3. The term 'Sri Lanka Tamils' refers to Tamils who migrated to Sri Lanka from the southern coastal areas of India several centuries ago. They settled in the northern and eastern coastal belts of the country, where they are heavily concentrated today.
4. Estate Tamils were not issued with NICs when they were introduced in the early 1970s because they were considered non-citizens. After 1988, when citizenship rights were restored, they began to be issued with NICs. In order to obtain an NIC, however, the applicant has to submit his or her birth certificate and a letter from the *gram sevak* of the area of residence. Many of these workers did not have birth certificates and there were no GSs in the estate areas. Even today, many of them do not possess NICs, although a letter from the estate superintendent is now accepted for the purpose of issuing IDs.
5. More recent estimates put the number of persons killed in the civil war at 60,000.
6. HDI levels for each country indicate how far a country has to go to attain certain defined goals to achieve a high quality of life—an average life span of 85 years, universal access to education, and a decent level of income. The closer a country's HDI is to one, the less the remaining distance that country has to travel. In 1994, Sri Lanka's HDI was 0.704, ranking 97 among countries surveyed.
7. The main difference between NGOs and People's Societies is that the former work for others, while the latter work to develop their own communities—

either through community-wide membership or more specific membership groups, such as women or farmers.

REFERENCES

Abeyasekara, C. and **S. Bastian.** *Structural Adjustment Policies in Sri Lanka: A Critical Evaluation—A study for the NGO-WB Committee* (Colombo: Social Scientists Association, 1993).

Annual Reports of Satyodaya, various years.

Beckford, L. *Persistent Poverty: Underdevelopment in Plantation Economics of the Third World* (London: OUP, 1972).

de Silva, S.B. *The Political Economy of Underdevelopment* (London: Routledge and Kegan Paul, 1982).

Fernando, A. and **Henry de Mel.** NGOs in Sri Lanka: An Introduction. Water Supply & Sanitation Decade Service (Colombo: NGO 1991).

Gunasinghe, N. 'Ethnic Conflict in Sri Lanka: Perception and Solution', in C. Abeysekara, and N. Gunasinghe (eds.) *Facets of Ethnicity in Sri Lanka* (Colombo: Social Scientists Association, 1987).

Korten, D. 'Third Generation NGO Strategies: A Key to People-centred Development', *World Development* 15, 1987.

MIRJE, 1981. *The Year of Racial Violence* (Colombo: MIRJE, 1983).

NARESA (The Natural Resources, Energy and Science Authority of Sri Lanka). *Natural Resources of Sri Lanka: Conditions and Trends.* (Colombo: NARESA, 1991).

Phadnis, U. *Ethnicity and Nation-Building in South Asia.* (New Delhi: Sage Publications, 1990).

Samarajeewa, A. and **G. Palaniappan.** 'Satyodaya Evaluation Report', 1993.

Satyodaya, 1997. 'Community Organisation and Community Development', Programme Proposal, 1998–2001.

Sansoni Commission Report. 'Report of the Presidential Commission of Inquiry into the Incidents which took place between 13th August and 15th September 1977', Sessional Paper No. VII, 1980.

Warnapala, W.A.W. and **D.E. Woodsworth.** *Monograph Series No. 22*, Centre for Developing Area Studies, McGill University. 1987.

World Bank, 1992. 'Sri Lanka: Strengthened Adjustment for Growth and Poverty Reduction', Report No. 10079-CE. South Asia Country Department III, 8 January 1992.

———- 1994. Sri Lanka: Poverty Assessment Report No. 13431-CE, Washington D.C.: World Bank Country Development III, South Asian Region.

4

The Experience of Sahayi: Capacity-Building for Sustainable Development

Gregory Placid

PART I: THE SOUTH INDIAN CONTEXT

The Capacity-Building Initiative

The dawn of the new millennium 2001 AD coincided with the tenth anniversary of Sahayi's entry into participatory development work—10 years of service in the capacity-building of civil society groups in Kerala, South India. Sahayi (or the Centre for Collective Learning and Action) began with hardly any financial resources and only a handful of individuals with capacity-building expertise and exposure to the NGO and voluntary development organisation (VDO) sector in the area, having identified its niche in the empowerment of small NGOs and VDOs working for the social and economic uplift of disadvantaged communities. The focus of Sahayi has since been to further the cause of participatory sustainable development by empowering civil society actors in Kerala, one of India's smallest and economically less developed states.

The invitation extended by the Commonwealth Foundation to share the experience of Sahayi in its capacity-building endeavours offers us the opportunity to seek feedback from our target constituencies about the efficacy of our programmes, and also make a general assessment of the outcome of our efforts and shortcomings.

Since January 1991, Sahayi has been involved in a wide range of capacity-building initiatives such as: perspective-building workshops; skill-development training; awareness-raising seminars; policy research and advocacy; information dissemination; consultancy and intensive support; and publication and networking.

Feedback from our target constituency indicates that our efforts have positively enhanced the capacities of individuals and groups, leading to empowerment and creativity among some of the civil society actors in the state. What follows is an attempt to document the dynamics of this process of empowerment and its consequences.

Historical Evolution

The empowerment mission of Sahayi perhaps evolved, at least partially, from my own initial exposure to the lives of the poor and the downtrodden, as well as to those groups and individuals who worked to improve their conditions.

I was initiated into social work through the NSS or National Service Scheme (a scheme to harness the unused energies of the university youth into nation-building activities) of the Indian government while I was an undergraduate student in 1972. As a student volunteer and leader of this forum, I worked among fishermen, who are among the most downtrodden people in India. Financial problems in the family forced me to discontinue my postgraduate studies in economics and join the service of the state government in a junior position in the Department of Tribal Welfare, created for the development of tribal people. This brought me into direct contact with the economically and socially most backward people in Indian society.

After eventually completing my Masters degree, I joined Cochin University as a co-ordinator of their continuing- and distance-education programmes. Subsequently, I joined the Centre for Development Studies as a Research Associate. Through this assignment, I gained wider exposure to the developmental issues pertaining to different sections of our society. One of my major assignments was a research study on the NGO and VDO sector in Kerala. This was my first encounter with NGOs and voluntary organisations in the state. This exposure eventually led to an invitation to Work with the Trivandrum District Fishermen's Federation (TDFF), an apex body of 30 grass-roots co-operative societies of the fishermen in the southernmost districts of Kerala. I accepted the invitation and worked with them for a year. In the meantime, I had also established a voluntary organisation (the West Kallada Social Welfare Society) and had started organising training programmes for unemployed youth in order to prepare them for competitive examinations and job interviews.

The Genesis of Sahayi

During my service at the TDFF, we initiated a process of developing a state-level network of secular voluntary organisations. I was one of the founding members of this informal network and also functioned as its organising secretary. It was initially called Voluntary Action Network India (VANI) – Kerala Chapter, and was later registered as a charitable organisation in 1994 with the new name Kerala Voluntary Agencies League (KAVAL).

The problem of limited capacity and lack of accessibility to information among the secular and small voluntary organisations in the state regularly came up for discussion in the meetings and consultations organised for the formation of the network. There was a consensus that something needed to be done to enhance the capacities of the personnel in the voluntary sector. Some participants emphasised that the network organisation should take up the challenge of providing capacity-building services. Apart from myself, some others, including NGO leaders such as K. Viswanathan (Mitraniketan), Eugene Culas (TDFF) and Professor T.S.N. Pillai (retired professor of Loyola College and a professional management consultant of NGOs) felt that there had to be a separate organisational entity to address the capacity-building needs of voluntary organisations. Our conviction was that the central role of the network would be advocacy for the cause of the voluntary sector in the state, but we also anticipated that the organisation might have specific kinds of problems, leading to potential conflicts with the state administration, funding agencies, and so on. Naturally, this would not be conducive to a climate for capacity-building activities, which require understanding and co-operation with these agencies.

This idea was shared with Dr Rajesh Tandon and his team at PRIA, New Delhi—one of the pioneering regional support organisations in capacity-building and a promoter of the philosophy of participation. Thereafter, it was decided that the KAVAL network should limit its activities to establishing working relationships and advocacy, and that a new organisation should be established for addressing the needs of capacity-building. And so Sahayi—the Centre for Collective Learning and Action—was formally registered in end-1990, although its activities began in earnest only in the beginning of 1991. The initial programmes were conducted with the collaboration of PRIA, whose support has strengthened Sahayi over the years.

Any organisation with the mission of capacity-building among NGOs and VDOs in Kerala was perceived to be an unviable proposition in the early 1990s, and Sahayi was greeted with characteristic scepticism by several organisations that did not recognise the need for capacity-building. While Sahayi's leaders and activists were deemed enlightened, their only perceived problem was lack of funds. Incidentally, when Sahayi arrived on the scene, most of the international funding agencies were withdrawing from Kerala.

The social service societies of the Christian churches and similar organisations had traditionally understood their main role to be that of distribution of charity to the poor and needy—'the beneficiaries'. All that was expected of a voluntary activist was concern for the poor and a willingness to work without being paid. The NGO/VDO sector was, to a considerable extent, negatively predisposed towards Sahayi, and the Church-based organisations initially kept aloof as all the founding members of Sahayi were self-professed 'secularists'.

The prominent secular NGOs of the time did not expect much from a small team of youngsters with limited NGO experience. Training people for the voluntary sector in Kerala was the prerogative of a few consultants who were associated with some funding agencies and helped the NGOs and VDOs to organise 'animation programmes'. A small VDO team normally consisted of one or two social workers with barely any training, since access to funding sources was felt to be their greatest need.

In a country like India, where large sections of the population live in abject poverty, non-governmental development organisations have the mission of facilitating collective action by local communities. The social activists who facilitate this process need to possess considerable skills. In order to empower the people, they need to build their own capacities.

Sahayi had its own inherent limitations, such as paucity of resources. But counted among its assets were a clear mission and a small, committed team with capacity-building experience. Financial support for a few specific training programmes was provided by PRIA. From such humble beginnings, Sahayi set out on its mission of capacity-building for the benefit of a large number of small- and medium-sized NGOs and VDOs as well as the communities they served.

Vision and Programmes

Sahayi strives to create a just, participatory and self-sustainable society. This, it believes, can be achieved only through equitable interaction and the redistribution of power among the various constituents of society. Power has been ruthlessly appropriated by certain sections of the population, resulting in the impoverishment and powerlessness of the rest. This social imbalance needs to be remedied through purposeful social action, of which enlightened intervention by civil society groups could be considered a major component. To this end, civil society groups need to be equipped with clarity of vision and capacities for action. In one word, they have to be 'empowered'.

Empowerment involves the expansion of personal capability and choice, which increases a person's ability to exercise choices free of hunger, want and deprivation. It also increases one's opportunity to participate in decision-making processes that affect one's own life.

Having formulated its vision through an analysis of the prevailing socio-economic situation, Sahayi set out to map its course of action. Around the central theme of empowerment, various programmes were designed, as shown in the following chart:

Empowerment through capacity-building is achieved by:

- development of management and job-oriented skills
- strengthening local self-governance
- information dissemination
- awareness generation
- self-development
- promotion and strengthening of self-help groups
- promotion of eco-friendly production
- publication
- participatory research and evaluation
- advocacy
- networking

The Relevance and Role of Civil Society Organisations

The National Scenario:　India is the seventh largest country in the world, with a land area of 3.287 million sq km. It is bordered by the Arabian Sea on the west, the Bay of Bengal on the east, and the Indian Ocean on the south. The border nations are Pakistan and Afghanistan to the west, Bangladesh and Myanmar to the east, and Nepal, Bhutan, and China to the north.

India has the second highest population in the world at over 1 billion. The Indian people belong to several different ethnic groups, and a variety of religious groups such as Hindus (83 per cent), Muslims (11 per cent), Christians (3 per cent) and Sikhs (2 per cent). The people of India speak 14 major languages and more than 1,000 minor languages and dialects.

The country has a large economy in terms of its GDP. But because of its large population, India has one of the lowest per capita GDP, and poverty is fairly widespread. Agriculture provides about a third of India's national income, with about 60 per cent of India's workers earning a living by farming. The health conditions of Indians are generally poor, and the country has a high mortality rate, partly due to poor diet and living conditions. Furthermore, a sizeable portion of the Indian population is illiterate.

The nation has a federal structure and consists of 28 states and seven union territories. Since Independence, it has followed a parliamentary democratic governance mechanism in which the President is the head of the state and the Prime Minister is the head of the government. Although the states are essential elements in Indian federal governance, there has been a strong tendency towards an accumulation of power at the centre. As centralised planning and implementation of projects proved ineffective, there was a corresponding movement towards a decentralised approach of administration, planning, and implementation.

With the enactment of the 73 rd (Panchayati Raj Act for Rural Governance) and 74 th (Nagarpalika Act for Urban Governance) Constitution Amendment Acts of 1992, the Indian government initiated a process of democratic decentralisation at the local level. The Panchayati Raj Act established a three-tier governance structure at the district, block and village levels.

Though independent India has a history of local self-governance, traditionally called panchayats (institutions of self-governance for rural areas), these institutions did not have a constitutional status. Through the new Act, the nation has succeeded in conferring constitutional status on Panchayati Raj Institutions (PRIs). Subject to the provisions of this Amendment, all states (except Bihar and Jammu and Kashmir) created suitable Acts to enable PRIs to function as institutions of self-governance through the devolution of necessary powers and responsibilities.

The Act paved the way for a new era of local self-governance, with characteristic features such as: decentralisation of power; the constitution of gram sabhas (village assemblies which meet occasionally to prioritise needs, propose development programmes to the panchayat samiti and identify beneficiaries); widening of the social base (through one-third reservation for women and Scheduled Castes and Scheduled Tribes); widening the functional jurisdiction of the PRIs; ensuring financial support (through the formation of a Finance Commission); guaranteeing elections every five years; and constitutionalising micro-level development planning. This new administrative system provided immense opportunities for decentralised bottom-up planning by ensuring the participation of local citizens in the planning, implementation and evaluation of development projects.

The NGO Scenario: India has a rich heritage of voluntary action, starting with 19th century movements against social evils such as untouchability and child marriage, through the nationalist and Independence movement. Combining social action with political action, the voluntary action movement in India has evolved through the decades, occasionally shifting its focus of interest and activity but retaining its essential spirit.

The 1990s witnessed unprecedented growth and development in the voluntary sector, with a large diversification of activities into specialised areas of research, policy advocacy, gender, environment and legal action. Voluntary organisations have increasingly gained in importance and have earned the approbation of both the citizens and the government.

The growing visibility of NGOs has provoked a series of associated responses. Major international and national development agencies, planners, ideologists and theoreticians have had to contend with the NGOs, their roles, positions, behaviour and dynamics—a phenomenon that had been largely missing till a decade ago. Most bilateral agencies engaged in providing development aid have started including NGOs within their framework. The same could be said of multilateral institutions and, in recent years, such bodies as the World Bank. National governments across the length and breadth of the world have had to deal with the growing visibility of NGOs, in varying degrees. (PRIA 1991: 62)

In India, as in the world at large, the NGOs are fast becoming the third sector. This means that their roles and responsibilities are growing, as are the challenges they face. The challenges faced by the voluntary sector stem from the following national issues:

- a growing disparity between the rich and the poor
- the ineffectiveness of the state machinery in dealing with all the issues
- the negative influence of globalisation, which invokes a qualitative shift towards a global economic system based on a consolidated global marketplace for production, distribution and consumption
- the increasing trend of human rights violations
- socio-political instability
- natural calamities
- the need for strengthening local self-governance

In order to face these challenges and play its role effectively, the voluntary sector is undergoing a transformation characterised by an increasing trend of professionalism. The voluntary organisations themselves need to upgrade their capacities as a prelude to building up the capacities of civil society groups.

The Kerala Scenario: Kerala lies along the south-western part of the west coast of peninsular India, with the Arabian sea on the west. It extends along the coast for 560 km, has a surface area of 38,863 sq km, and a population of about 31 million. Contrary to the pattern across India, in Kerala women outnumber men (1,058 women per 1,000 men). About 59.5 per cent of the population are Hindus, 21.5 per cent Muslims and 19 per cent Christians. Kerala is remarkable in several respects, but its natural beauty is perhaps its most striking feature, which has even lent it the epithet 'God's own country'.

Kerala's economy is beset with problems. Though it is blessed with natural resources, it lags behind in economic development. Its per capita income and growth rate are very low as compared with other Indian states. A growing population, shortage of agricultural land, the poor status of industries, severe unemployment and social unrest could be considered the main impediments to Kerala's economic progress.

Kerala has been heavily dependent on the income repatriated by migrant workers, particularly in the Gulf countries. For the past several years, the remittances of migrant workers have decreased and a large number of migrant workers have returned home. With a deteriorating agriculture sector, a small and stagnant industrial sector, and a declining repatriated income, the status of Kerala's economy is precarious.

Kerala's economy today is an example of poor vision and short-sighted planning. Populist welfare measures of successive coalition governments which competed for popularity and neglected to formulate long-term plans based on equity and ecological harmony, have driven the state to the brink of economic disaster. Among other negative developments are environmental ruin, corruption among politicians and bureaucrats and marginalisation of the weaker sections of society such as the Scheduled Castes, Scheduled Tribes and fishermen, who collectively make up a sizeable chunk of the state population. The result is that life has become increasingly difficult for the poor and labouring classes.

However, the position of Kerala in the social service sector is relatively strong. The state has achieved a high level of literacy, and its healthcare and education sectors are quite strong. It may be noted that in all these sectors, civil society groups and movements have made a substantial contribution.

Civil Society Groups: Civil society organisations (CSOs) have been an integral part of contemporary Kerala society, and comprise a host of associations around which society voluntarily organises itself. They include NGOs; gender, language, cultural and religious groups; charities; co-operatives, community development organisations; trade unions; environmental groups; professional associations; academic and policy institutions; and media outlets. The contribution made by CSOs to the building of modern Kerala becomes evident when one considers the service rendered by such agencies and movements as the Christian churches, the Sree Narayana Dharmaparipalana Sangam, the Nair Service Society and the early Communist movement.

Among the NGOs/VDOs in the state, there are large agencies with abundant resources, infrastructure and professionals; medium-sized agencies with a fair amount of resources, minimum infrastructure and personnel; and small organisations with hardly any resources, infrastructure or skilled personnel.

Initially, Sahayi's capacity-building services were directed exclusively to small- and medium-sized development-oriented secular voluntary organisations, with a special focus on women's organisations. Later, the sphere of activity was extended to include most of the CSOs. However, considering their development potential, priority is given even now to small- and medium-sized development-oriented organisations, movements and groups. The fact is that, if these groups are equipped with a proper vision, mission, strategy and resources, they can play critical roles in advocacy and social action for the benefit of the weaker, marginalised sections of the population, filling in the gaps left unattended by the state and the business sectors, and catalysing sustainable development processes.

The mission and strategy of Sahayi's programmes have been formulated based on an assessment of the capacity-building requirements of NGOs and other citizen groups, and address the following needs and problems.

At the Organisational Level:

- Limited information and knowledge base
- Lack of clarity on organisational mission and strategy
- Leadership problems
- Lack of internal training facilities and inability to attend external training programmes
- Lack of competence in programme management
- Lack of awareness of and accessibility to sources of funds
- Lack of co-ordination and networking among civil society groups

At the Community Level:

- Passivity or apathy towards socio-political and economic issues
- Insensitivity of policy-makers towards the needs of disadvantaged sections of society
- Low participation of women in decision-making

Feedback: For the last 10 years, Sahayi has been involved in capacity-building interventions among the civil society actors in Kerala. An attempt was made recently to obtain feedback from some of the civil society groups to ascertain the impact of Sahayi's interventions. Their responses have been documented in the following pages.

PART II: THE EMPOWERING PROCESS AND ITS OUTCOME

From the Individual to the Community

K. Ambujakshan, a young man of 32 years, is the founder–president of the Kerala Dalit Panthers, an informal organisation that promotes activism for the liberation and development of the oppressed Dalit community in Kerala. The organisation currently has a membership of around 0.1 million Dalits in various parts of the state.

Even as a boy, Ambujakshan—reminiscent of Ambedkar, the champion and prophet of the Dalits in India—was intensely conscious of the discrimination practised against members of his community by the upper castes. His revolutionary fervour was kept ablaze through his educational years, and while a student of engineering in the Regional Engineering College, Kozhikode, he founded the Kerala Dalit Panthers in 1988. The organisation was meant to be an effective response to the disunity and lethargy of his community in the face of the burning problems of marginalisation and humiliation meted out to peace-loving and hard-working Dalits, who had had a glorious past before they had been subjugated and suppressed by the invading powers.

Ambujakshan's first contact with Sahayi came in 1996 during the first phase of the Training of Trainers (henceforth ToT) course conducted at Kumily. He liked the innovative course, and went on to attend the next two phases as well. The ToT programme aims to develop a group of participatory trainers in the state. The trained NGO leaders are, in turn, expected to offer participatory training to various civil society groups in their operational areas. The ToT programme achieves these objectives by increasing the knowledge and skill of the participants in the philosophy of participatory training and small group processes in the context of learning, designing and organising participatory training programmes; and in choosing the appropriate training methods. It also provides an opportunity for the self-development of prospective trainers.

Participatory training methodology is rooted in the belief that people can develop through their own actions. This approach encourages participants to see themselves as a source of information and knowledge about the real world. When they are encouraged to work with the knowledge they have gained from their own experience, they become capable of developing strategies to change their immediate situation.

The methods used included group discussions, lectures, simulations, case studies, role playing, practical exercises, etc.

The training experience resulted in remarkable changes in Ambujakshan's life. Participatory training proved to be a revelation for him, and enabled him to equate his life's ambition with the development of his community. A charismatic leader, Ambujakshan was also a very successful organiser who had earned the respect and love of his people within a short span of time. However, he felt there was something amiss in the way he communicated and took decisions. The ToT provided him with valuable insights into his own experience and opened up before him the world of participatory approaches. It slowly dawned on Ambujakshan that, even while avowedly denouncing all forms of oppression and subjugation, he might have been unconsciously duplicating the patterns of the oppressors by imposing his own views and preferences on others, in a benevolent but nevertheless dictatorial fashion.

The 21-day intensive learning experience helped him change aspects of his outlook and attitude. It rid him of his own prejudices and egoism, and in the process generated tremendous amounts of creative energy. Emerging from the training with a new vision, he shared his new-found knowledge with his colleagues and advised them to undergo the same type of training offered by Sahayi. Consequently, fresh activist recruits from the Kerala Dalit Panthers attended a variety of Sahayi's training programmes, including the ToT, all of which are characterised by a strong undercurrent of participatory methodology. The cumulative result was that the functioning of the Kerala Dalit Panthers had changed from an authoritarian style to a democratic one, with shared collective leadership, enhancement of capacities, broadening of vision, greater tolerance, pluralism, flexibility, co-operation, team work and innovation. The process did not stop with the team of organisers, but spread to the masses as well, for in all their meetings and interactions with the people, the organisers carried with them the spirit of a newfound inner freedom and creativity. The result was that the organisation began to grow both in number and quality of participation, thereby making the movement more effective. Unfettered by dogma, social determinism, exclusivity and the like, the members began to experience a new vitality and confidence that, in turn, opened the doors of the movement to larger sections of the community. 'As a result, we could get the intellectuals into our movement,' says Ambujakshan, reminiscing about the beneficial organisational changes that occurred as a result of the exposure to participatory approaches.

One of the results of the attitudinal change of the Kerala Dalit Panthers was its decision to branch out into other areas of activity besides political mobilisation, such as economic and cultural operations. For instance, the organisation started promoting self-help groups among women and registered a new organisational outfit called the Janata Development Society. A musical troupe called 'The Black Voice', was launched with a view to complementing the revolutionary fervour of the group with inspiring melodies. In order to address the problems of illiteracy and low levels of education, they organised free tuition centres in their operational areas. The awareness that their daily socio-economic needs had to be met even as they struggled for the ultimate liberation of their people, was an important aspect of the lesson learnt by Ambujakshan and his friends. In a word, it could be said that a unidimensional, isolated movement was transformed into a multidimensional movement, ready to forge alliances with like-minded groups across the state.

From a purely agitational style of operation, the Kerala Dalit Panthers soon moved towards an approach that addressed the entire gamut of human and developmental issues in the community. The conviction that this would be better fulfilled not in isolation, but in collaboration with the rest of humanity led to their joining the Confederation of Human Rights Organisations, which began in 1997. Currently, Ambujakshan is its vice-chairman. Yet another welcome change is that more young people have risen up the ranks of leadership, and that the movement has slowly become feminised—increasing numbers of women have been joining the ranks of the organisation and wielding power in the decision-making process.

On analysis, one realises that what had happened to Ambujakshan and his group was nothing short of a psychological revolution, which led to positive changes in both individual and collective behaviour. Understandably, the Dalits had been angry and resentful with the structures and forces that had oppressed them through the centuries. This only strengthened their resolve to combat the forces of injustice and oppression to ensure that they regained their identity and lived with dignity, on par with the rest of society. These were noble intentions, but how was this goal to be achieved?

The original strategy of the organisation was to protest vehemently against the unjust order and clamour for justice. Pent-up anger had clouded their vision so completely that political agitation seemed the only form of action open to them. The exposure to ToT in a relaxed and informal setting opened their eyes and hearts. Several sessions of sharing and group interaction in a cordial, non-threatening atmosphere enabled them to understand themselves not only as historically conditioned objects capable only of reaction, but also as historically evolving subjects, who could change themselves and the world around them through conscious action and interaction.

The participants learnt to see and accept human beings as psychosocial complexities. They understood that lasting changes could occur only through complex, prolonged and sustained processes and that there was more to social living than political action. Authentic social change cannot be brought about mechanically. For any revolution to happen, individuals have to become conscious and empowered through experience. The realisation that the most effective weapons for fighting injustice are participatory and holistic approaches slowly percolated through the participants' consciousness. The participants relaxed and became convinced that beyond long-term political ambitions, people have material needs, which a committed activist cannot turn a blind eye to. In sum, the process of self-understanding led to the understanding and integration of the group and the community. The self-confidence gained by individuals has resulted in the empowerment of a community.

Promoting Skills

The major problem with most small- and medium-sized NGOs and VDOs is paucity of funds and programmes. International funding agencies often support well-established organisations, while new and emerging VDOs are ignored. One of the first major activities of Sahayi was to identify funding agencies within the country that provided specific developmental funds for agencies in the non-governmental sector. Several government-sponsored agencies that had provided funds for grass-roots level development work were contacted by Sahayi. Their funding norms and procedures were studied and documented, and the relevant information published in the *Sahayi Newsletter* which was then widely circulated within Kerala.

Many small- and medium-sized organisations realised that they did not have the skills required to comply with the demands of the funding agencies. Several organisations began to contact Sahayi for advice and guidance with regard to the preparation of projects. First, maintaining proper accounts and records was a basic requirement for receiving programme funds from any funding agency. NGOs and VDOs in general, and small organisations in particular, had several constraints in this respect, for they lacked accounting and documentation skills. The request for help in programme planning, accounting, and documentation motivated Sahayi to offer training programmes in these areas. In addition to training programmes, Sahayi also offered intensive support to individual organisations.

This intervention created an impact at the grass-roots level. With the support of funding agencies, some organisations were able to implement health and sanitation programmes in the villages. Other organisations implemented income-generation programmes for the rural poor. Several women's organisations initiated saving and credit programmes for the benefit of hundreds of families.

Intensive Support

One of Sahayi's strategies has been to provide need-based consultancy services to small and nascent organisations. The story of how organisational development support from Sahayi transformed a movement has already been narrated in the case of Ambujakshan and his team. The objective of such an intervention was to make the organisation aware of its particular situation, redefine its vision and mission, and strengthen its capacity for formulating programmes in response to the needs of its target groups. This was achieved through a combination of efforts including skill development training, consultancy and information sharing. The package of need-based consultancy services rendered by Sahayi to various voluntary organisations covered the following areas:

- analysing organisational vision and mission
- streamlining organisational structures and systems
- formulating organisational objectives and strategies
- formulating feasible and viable programmes
- providing guidance for introducing proper accounting and book-keeping systems
- assisting in the preparation of annual reports and minutes

The Story of Santhigram

Santhigram is a people-centred VDO working in the Kottukal panchayat of the Thiruvananthapuram district. From the very start, Santhigram was exposed to the capacity-building influence of Sahayi. The first programme that Pankajakshan, the director of Santhigram, attended was the programme planning and budgeting course. The objective of the programme was to provide a perspective on organisational vision, mission and strategies, and to enhance the capacity for programme planning and project development. Subsequently, Pankajakshan also attended the ToT and Sahayi organisation development programmes.

Beginning with Pankajakshan, almost all the activists of the organisation participated in one or more of Sahayi's training programmes, including training in leadership and motivation, organisation management, participatory rural appraisal, programme planning and budgeting, and public advocacy. A close look at the development of Santhigram and its activities over the years will give us an idea of the nature of the impact of Sahayi's capacity-building endeavours.

Making good use of Sahayi's input, which included a consultancy in organisation development, Santhigram was able to reorient and revitalise itself. Although the organisation had been established with a broad vision, the vision itself lacked clarity and close linkage with the programmes. Not only was documentation insubstantial, and development of capacities related only to the facilitation of group processes, even exercises such as report writing, effective communication, planning programmes and preparing budgets were beyond Santhigram's abilities, and had to be undertaken using outside resources.

Gradually, positive changes on all these fronts occurred in Santhigram. Over the years, it has become a prominent voluntary organisation in Kerala. In fact, today the organisation has gained a national reputation as an effective organisation which promotes people's development initiatives, following Gandhi's path of peaceful and participatory approach. Santhigram organises and conducts various kinds of participatory training for the benefit of organisations and groups throughout Kerala.

From a grass-roots organisation interested in people's development, Santhigram has emerged as a movement desired and valued *by* the people. Hitherto there had been a gap, however tenuous, between the organisation's goals and people's aspirations. The organisation meant well, and the people co-operated, but they did not feel that it was *their* organisation and consequently there was some emotional distance between the two.

The most important factor in the development and evolution of Santhigram has been the bridging of this distance between the organisation and the local poor, whose development has formed Santhigram's rationale for existence. The happy result is that through varied experiences of learning, interacting, serving, struggling and winning, not only has this gap has been bridged over time, but the relationship between the organisation and the people it proposes to serve has also improved significantly. 'Previously we had to coax people to attend the meetings, and even so the attendance would be very thin. Now they come without being asked and insist that we conduct programmes for them. They want to ensure that we are present in their community meetings,' said Pankajakshan. He felt fulfilled that finally the people had accepted Santhigram as 'their own organisation'.

The capacity-building programme at Santhigram had its impact on the neighbourhood community. A specific case in point is the Dalit community in Chinantevila colony near Chappath in Kottukal village. This Dalit settlement epitomised social problems, especially acute poverty, low level of awareness and disunity, which were manifest in illicit liquor trade, alcoholism, drunken brawls and wife-beating.

Santhigram had, from the beginning, endeavoured to interact with this community and help them in whatever way possible. Accordingly some remedial measures, such as alternative income-generation activities, were initiated. The women were motivated and assisted in taking up coir-making as an alternative source of income. At first the people's response was half-hearted, but participation improved with time. Even so, there remained a distance, because in the eyes of the people, Santhigram signified a set of do-gooders, who were well-meaning, but who were merely conducting a programme of which the locals were the beneficiaries.

This attitude changed gradually as Santhigram introduced 'participatory strategic planning' into the community. Through prolonged, arduous sessions of group learning, sharing, deliberation, analysis and planning that involved the entire Chinantevila colony, the people were able to identify and realise solutions to their problems by themselves. They even evolved a code of conduct for members of the community and set up mechanisms for monitoring and punishing the offenders. For instance, it was decided that after a certain time in the evening, no outsider would be allowed to enter the colony. This was to prevent the sale of alcohol and other nefarious activities. It was also decided that differences between individuals and families would henceforth be settled in community meetings, steering clear of quarrels and court procedures. Steps were also initiated to improve the economic conditions of the families.

The exercises of participatory strategic planning enabled the people of the Chinantevila colony lead a peaceful, harmonious life. These exercises, which lasted for months, were effectively facilitated by Santhigram's resourceful team of social workers, who were, in due course of time, accepted as members of the Dalit community in Chinantevila colony. To sum up, the consistent and creative use of participatory approaches resulted in remarkable changes for both the voluntary organisation and the people. It is pertinent to note here that Sahayi had not only sown the seeds of this participatory approach to development, but also continued to keep vigil and nurture the 'seedlings' through a variety of interventions over the years.

Organisational Transformation

Transparency and accountability are essential to any civil society organisation. However, most voluntary organisations often fail to maintain proper accounts, reports and other relevant documents. Sahayi's bookkeeping, accountancy, reporting and documentation programmes have helped several such organisations to streamline their internal systems and procedures.

Arangamkoly Vikasana Samiti in Kannur is a classic example of how proper documentation has transformed a hitherto small, dormant voluntary organisation with very few activities into an active voluntary development organisation. Gopinatha Pillai, the chief functionary of this organisation, had been educated only up to the primary school level, and was initially barely aware of book-keeping and documentation procedures. After attending a series of Sahayi's training programmes, he streamlined his accounting and book-keeping practices, and also acquired some skill in the preparation of reports and documentation. Proper documentation consequently helped the organisation obtain development aid from reputed agencies for several programmes.

Sahayi's capacity-building programmes have often led to the radical transformation of organisations and granted substantial economic benefits to the community the latter served. The Sandhya Development Society, Pala in Kottayam district which was established in

1981 as the Sandhya Arts and Sports Club, by a team of enterprising youth led by K.C. Thankachan, is a good case in point. The vision and goals of the organisation are self-evident, viz. the promotion of arts and sports among youth, and this is what it had been doing for over a decade—until 1993, when Thankachan, the leader of the group, attended a training programme conducted by Sahayi. Although he was full of optimistic enthusiasm, his vision was clearly narrow. Fortunately, his interaction with Sahayi did not end with a two-day leadership and motivation training programme but was the first of a long series of capacity-building interactions with Sahayi, including visits, consultancy, follow-up training, information dissemination, etc. Following in Thankachan's footsteps, groups of his organisation's members attended several training sessions. The cumulative effect of these sessions resulted in the transformation of the organisation as a whole from a mere youth club that promoted arts and sports to a well-planned VDO with a clear-cut vision, mission, strategies, objectives and activities.

Initially, members of the team attended Sahayi's leadership training programmes. With the development of self-confidence, greater awareness, leadership and communication skills, the team gained in dynamism. With the help of additional inputs from Sahayi on programme planning and budgeting, they were able to develop innovative programmes and projects on their own.

The first thing that Sandhya Arts and Sports Club did was to change its name. Subsequently, it started several women's self-help groups (SHGs) and linked them to its informal banking system. It also offered an array of programmes, which included skills training for women, catering units, restaurants managed by women, a bakery unit, and a training and production centre, which sold washing soap, ayurvedic toilet soap and toys. In this way, the organisation generated employment for over 500 people. Today, Thankachan feels gratified that he has been able to organise the movement on such a large scale and has caught the attention of the local people, the panchayat and the government—all of which, he acknowledges with gratitude, has been made possible by Sahayi's capacity-building support.

Over the years, Sahayi has extended its capacity-building training support to 5,558 voluntary or development workers belonging of 2,611 VDOs and NGOs in Kerala, as shown in Table 4.1. The actual number of organisations may be less, since the figures show multiple counting with respect of several organisations.

Table 4.1

Capacity-building training interventions (1991–2002)

Year	No. of programmes	No. of VDOs that participated	No. of participants
1991	2	30	65
1992	6	75	150
1993	15	205	450
1994	22	290	620
1995	26	351	718
1996	16	225	460
1997	22	328	591
1998	22	345	700
1999	20	371	853
2000	16	231	411
2001	7	100	325
2002	8	60	215
Total	182	2,611	5,558

Strengthening Women's Groups

The government, the voluntary sector and the international community have, in recent times, attached a great deal of importance to the empowerment of women, particularly in marginalised communities. Sahayi, conscious of its mission and sensitive to emerging social trends, has accordingly included among its activities components of capacity-building for women's organisations and informal SHGs, which normally comprise 20 members and are mainly involved in thrift and credit programmes. These capacity-building measures include perspective-building orientation and leadership development programmes and courses in SHG management, consultancy and counselling. The overall objective behind these interventions has been to re-organise the above groups into strong women's institutions that cater to the needs of society while retaining a special focus on women's and children's issues. Table 4.2 indicates the support provided by Sahayi to these groups.

The Kuttanad Vikasana Samiti is a VDO situated in Alappuzha district. The story of this VDO's metamorphosis begins with Thressiamma, the community co-ordinator, who attended Sahayi's organisation management training in 1994. It was a watershed, according to

Table 4.2

Strengthening SHGs—leadership and management training support

Major beneficiary organisations	No. of programmes	No. of groups	No. of participants
Sandhya Development Society, Kottayam	10	221	800
Sevasram, Ernakulam	5	150	250
Kuttanad Vikasana Samiti, Alappuzha	6	180	274
FREED, Alappuzha	9	457	430
Society of Love, Kasaragod	11	80	907
Karshaka Reksha Samiti, Kannur	5	90	285
ADPs of World Vision (Various Districts)	30	250	1,800
Others	55	700	3,200
Total	131	2,128	7,946

Thressiamma, not only in her outlook on development work but also in the direction and dynamism of the organisation. The initial training was followed by a series of other training programmes and support activities such as consultancy and information sharing, all of which focused on improving the management of the organisation through capacity-building of the personnel, and which eventually led to the re-structuring of the organisation along scientific lines.

Consequently, the samiti began to maintain records systematically, and reporting and accounting procedures were also streamlined. The organisation's sense of orientation and team spirit improved, and the team itself began to work with greater freedom and spontaneity. The SHG movement, which was the central concern of the organisation, grew in leaps and bounds. Previously, the objectives and activities of the SHGs had been narrowly confined to small savings and micro-credit, but now they extended into the wider horizon of social development. The SHGs became the nucleus of a collective endeavour to improve the quality of life of the village communities. Basing their vision on the perennial values of co-operation, friendship, and ecological harmony, the SHG movement surged into the lead with an integrated approach to development, implementing programmes of alternative income generation, environmental protection, integrated farming, etc.

Similar is the case of Sathi Chandrasekharan, secretary of Friends Women's Welfare, Muhamma, Alappuzha ever since its inception in 1996. In 1998, Sathi attended Sahayi's SHG Management training. She recalls:

We didn't know what to do, how to manage an SHG. We were not clear about our roles. We thought that the president and secretary were bigwigs who had to rule with an iron hand. So we decided everything for the group. There was no consultation. This dictatorial approach used to create bickering. Discontented members used to murmur and register their protest, but we didn't bother. However, this style of functioning changed after Sahayi's SHG management training. We became clearer about the nature and importance of SHG activity, and conscious of our roles and responsibilities. We shared our learning with the other members of the group. Now the members are keen that we continue as leaders.

The training by Sahayi opened up our mental horizons. We became convinced that we were all equals in the group, and we shared our thoughts with the rest of the group. This brought about unity and intimacy among the members of the group, and the level of co-operation dramatically improved. This new spirit of unity and collective responsibility was reflected in the management of the group. For instance, the repayment of loans became regular and punctual. Even the die-hard defaulters began to be punctual in repaying loans taken from the group. Now the members genuinely feel that the group belongs to them and that it is their sacred duty to make prompt repayment. The better functioning of the group has earned the appreciation of the public, who have started paying heed to the views of the SHG members. Even the panchayat members often consult us with regard to community development matters. The panchayat has entrusted us with the task of identifying the beneficiaries of individual panchayat schemes.

The new vitality of the group has led to the widening of our interests beyond the area of thrift and micro-credit. We started undertaking community service activities, like constructing a waiting shed and cleaning roads in collaboration with Iswarya Mahila Samajam, a local women's organisation. We felt that this was part of our responsibility to the community. As a result, the people began to trust us more and more. To cite an example, the panchayat failed to get the compliance of the beneficiaries in the construction of public latrines. We intervened and people co-operated.

Although Sahayi's leadership development programme lasts for only two to three days, it has been found to be highly effective in capacity-building. This training, with its focus on personality development, leadership qualities, communicative skills and group dynamics, stimulates the development of insights about the self and the group, leading to clarity of vision and enhancement of self-confidence. Sahayi's training is always flexible and adapts to the needs expressed by the group concerned. In the case of SHGs, elements of SHG management are also incorporated into the course. In the true spirit of participatory training, the final design of the course is fixed during the planning meeting with the trainee group.

As has been demonstrated in the cases of Thressiamma, Sathi Chandrasekharan and several others, what triggers the change most often is the discovery of self-worth, leading to self-confidence. It is diffidence that makes people aloof, withdrawn and antagonistic. Once the spark of self-confidence is ignited, it keeps growing through interactions and works its way into the group and then the community, generating waves of synergy and leading to systemic changes. Participatory training also facilitates the development of the spontaneity and uniqueness of the individual. The development potential of the SHG movement comes not only from its economic implications, but also from its psychological underpinnings, which promote self-development and creativity through open group interaction.

Strengthening the Local Self-Governance Institutions

India's local self-governance institutions (LSGIs), such as the village panchayats and the town and city nagarpalikas, are equipped with special powers and resources sanctioned by the 73rd and 74th Constitutional Amendments. Their objective of decentralisation of power and maximum participation of the people in the planning and implementation of development programmes is lofty and attractive, but is, in practice just the opposite of the professed goal. Power and resources are still monopolised by vested interest groups. The causes are several:

- the people are not enlightened and united enough to effectively demand their share of power;
- there is over-politicisation of local governance and resistance to change on the part of politicians and bureaucrats;
- the elected representatives barely possess the required perspectives or competence;
- the citizens are passive and lack motivation to participate in the process of governance.

The solution to these problems, therefore, lies in educating, empowering and mobilising the citizens and their elected representatives to demand and exercise power, as also in lobbying with the government and the policy-makers for policy changes and administrative reforms. In simple terms, it means capacity-building on the one hand and policy lobbying on the other.

This is what Sahayi has endeavoured to do, long before the State Act was passed in April 1994, and the government had even thought about the process of strengthening the PRIs. Sahayi sensed the importance and scope of the proposed amendments, heralding the beginning of a new era of local self-governance.

A Multidimensional Strategy

A multidimensional strategy was evolved by Sahayi for promoting good governance in democratic institutions at the grass-roots level. Towards this, a well-orchestrated array of programmes of awareness generation, skill development, policy research, consultancy, information dissemination, publication and networking were conducted in collaboration with like-minded voluntary organisations throughout the state. This Panchayati Raj Institutions-strengthening project became part of an all-India project by the Network of Collaborating Regional Support Organisations under the leadership of PRIA. This joint project, started in 1995, continues to this day and has produced a number of welcome results.

The concept of Panchayati Raj was universally welcomed as being a revolutionary and timely one. However, its successful implementation called for enormous efforts of capacity-building on the part of the people as well as the functionaries. After all, the radical change of an entire polity in its direction, attitude and practice is not possible without enlightened, systematic and sustained education and training. Although the government machinery, with its training institutes such as the Kerala Institute for Local Administration (KILA), had access to the required resources and manpower and also possessed good infrastructural facilities, it could handle only a fraction of the capacity-building requirement. Also, its approach provided little scope for attitudinal change and skill development. On the non-governmental side, there were hardly any agencies prepared and competent enough to enter this all-important sphere in the cause of the new Panchayati Raj.

This was a historic challenge, and Sahayi embraced it in earnest. Sahayi was already engaged in the sphere of capacity-building and had developed its expertise for effectively undertaking the task. But Sahayi's resource base was marginal in comparison with the government machinery (particularly with regard to finance). Even so, with the available resources, we conducted a variety of capacity-building programmes for the benefit of the local people (gram sabha members), the elected members and functionaries of the panchayats and the voluntary activists (see Table 4.3).

Thus far, Sahayi has provided perspective/capacity-building support to 50 panchayats, and another 100 panchayats have been covered through direct intervention and collaborating with partner organisations. But the information dissemination has reached all the 1,156 panchayats in the state, in addition to ensuring the availability of this information in NGOs, libraries, educational institutions and so on. The estimated readership of the *PRI News Bulletin* is about 5,000.

Table 4.3
PRI: Perspective-Building, Awareness and Training Programmes

Programmes	No. of participants								
	1994–95	1995–96	1996–97	1997–98	1998–99	1999–2000	2000–2001	2001–2002	Total
Leadership/management for PRI members	–	30	70	80	66	82	325	466	1,117
Women's leadership	–	50	80	160	295	500	459	300	1,844
Perspective-building awareness for citizens and PRI members	105	278	495	479	2,563	2,770	14,484	19,867	41,041
Seminars/consultations, interface with policy-makers, politicians, bureaucrats, academia, media and NGO leaders	–	481	279	210	238	370	180	830	2,588
ToT for NGO leaders and development actors	30	33	37	–	–	39	15	18	172

One of the important contributions made by Sahayi to the cause of the Panchayati Raj is the team of resource persons it has provided, who function as the mainstay for operations such as personnel training, planning and monitoring projects throughout Kerala.

A total of 100 trained leaders belonging to voluntary organisations currently function as resourcepersons at the state, district and panchayat levels. It has been observed, even by government officials and panchayat functionaries, that while most of the resourcepersons trained by the state government institutions dropped out, those trained by Sahayi continue to do excellent work.

Empowering for Participation

Sahayi's awareness-generation programmes started immediately after the Panchayati Raj Act was implemented in Kerala on 23 April 1994. The first programme for pre-election awareness was intended to make people aware of the concepts and ideas of grass-roots self-governance, and of the need to exercise their voting rights and participate in the political process. Several such programmes were conducted in different parts of the state. In all, more than 1,000 citizens participated in the pre-election awareness programmes and more than 3,000 people benefited from our information-sharing programmes through pamphlets and learning materials.

Some of the participants in Sahayi's pre-election awareness programmes are now elected leaders of the panchayats. Having participated in the pre-awareness programme they were seen to perform their duties better on the strength of the knowledge they had gained from it. It has been reported that the participants of our pre-awareness programmes have been involved in the post-election activities of the panchayats as well.

Strengthening Gram Sabhas

In view of the need for gram sabhas to play a vital role in the local governance mechanism, as also the need for people to participate creatively in the gram sabha meetings, Sahayi has been organising orientation programmes for reinforcing gram sabhas in almost every district in Kerala for the past five years.

There have been interesting instances of collective action by citizens who were motivated by Sahayi's orientation programmes. For example, in the Nedumbassery panchayat in Ernakulam district, where the panchayat samiti had manipulated the formation of *ayalkootams** by nominating members of the ruling political parties and giving them full control over beneficiary selection, the women members who attended Sahayi's orientation registered their protest. They demanded that the *ayalkootams* be democratically reorganised and that the malpractice by anti-social elements in the *ayalkootams* and *panchayat samitis* stopped, the *panchayat samiti* had no option but to reorganise the *ayalkootams* and conduct the beneficiary selection in a more transparent manner.

Participation in Good Governance

Odukkath Vijayanandan, the founder-leader of Anamritha Prasthanam in Perumkadavila in Thiruvananthapuram district, who is currently the president of the Perumkadavila gram panchayat, is another beneficiary of Sahayi's capacity-building programmes on the Panchayati Raj. From 1993 onwards, Vijayanandan and his group have worked in close association with Sahayi, availing of its capacity-building training and Panchayati Raj programmes. Vijayanandan participated in microplanning training and PRIs conducted by Sahayi in 1994. This was a

---

*An *ayalkootam* is an informal association of 25–50 families in a locality, constituted to increase their participation in local development activities.

two-phase programme intended to improve the participants' knowledge of the Panchayati Raj Act and skill in micro-planning, and to use the participatory rural appraisal method as an empowering process.

On returning from the training, Vijayanandan intensified his Panchayati Raj activities, and conducted a pioneering need-assessment survey of the panchayat. This was later submitted to the panchayat for formulating projects, and served as a basic document for planning development projects and schemes. Meanwhile, Vijayanandan contested the 1995 election as an independent candidate and was elected a panchayat member. Soon after, the panchayat council elected him their vice-president. As vice-president, Vijayanandan was admired by the people for his commitment and respected by his peers for his organisational abilities. Upon the sudden demise of the president, who happened to be his mentor, Vijayanandan was elected to the post. He discharges his duties efficiently and unassumingly to this day, to the satisfaction of the people and the panchayat council.

Gram Vikasana Samiti, a voluntary organisation in the West Ellery panchayat in Kasargod district, has been associated with Sahayi for seven years, and is one of the collaborating organisations in the Panchayati Raj project. K. P. Narayanan, its founder-leader, attended a seven-day residential ToT conducted in January 1996 in a village in West Kallada panchayat in Kollam district, which was attended by 33 representatives of voluntary organisations from different districts. Most of these representatives were then engaged by the People's Planning Campaign, initiated by the Government of Kerala. Narayanan was designated as a district resource person, and among the tasks assigned to him were activities such as facilitating the convening of the gram sabhas, informing and educating the people on various aspects of the panchayat and the People's Planning Campaign, and aiding and assisting the formulation of projects.

The training provided by Sahayi stood him in good stead, said Narayanan, adding that Sahayi's training proved to be more useful, comprehensive and practical, and the methods more participatory, than those offered by government institutions. Subsequently, Narayanan played a key role in the formulation of development projects for the West Ellery panchayat. He was made the joint convenor of the panchayat task force, which had to supervise the convening of gram sabhas, and the formulation and writing of projects. He was also the convenor of the Block Co-ordination Committee of Voluntary Organisations, which co-ordinated the work of 141 organisations, and whose network was greatly appreciated by the panchayat authorities. By recognising the contribution made by Narayanan and his group, the panchayat was, in effect, endorsing the role and importance of the voluntary sector itself.

Micro-planning Experiments

A total lack or low level of citizen participation in the planning and implementation of development projects has been identified as the root cause of the failure of development projects during the last 50 years of India's struggle for progress. The Panchayati Raj system was instituted to address this lacuna. The new law seeks to transfer to people at the grass roots the power to take vital decisions regarding their actual issues and priorities, the kind of activities to be undertaken to solve the issues, and the ways in which resources would be utilised to optimally improve their living conditions. This local-level participatory planning is the crux of Panchayati Raj.

Among the Indian states, only Kerala has produced a programme for promoting people's planning. This exercise, started in August 1996, was christened the People's Planning Campaign. Initially there were differences of opinion between the people and their leaders regarding the effectiveness of the programme, the motivation behind it and the methods used. However, the relevance and importance of promoting people's participation in the planning and implementation of development projects was never in doubt. Local people were seen to be in a better position to understand their specific needs and resources than the remote policy maker, and with a little technical support, they could become capable of planning and implementing programmes for their own development.

Sahayi was way ahead of other organisations in Kerala in understanding the importance of promoting people's planning in the panchayats as the central activity for ensuring equitable and sustainable development. As mentioned earlier, it has been offering orientation and training in participatory planning methods such as participatory rural appraisal to voluntary organisations since 1994.

Sahayi also adopted a two-fold approach to the promotion of people-centred micro-planning. This involved direct intervention in a village, followed by the provision of technical support to collaborating organisations to conduct similar experiments in their own areas. The West

Kallada panchayat in Kollam district was chosen to demonstrate the process of direct intervention, and several organisations were then identified for promotional activities.

This programme was initiated in 1996 after a series of orientation and training exercises. Armed with a sound theoretical grounding and basic practical skills, the team of facilitators began the experiment with a participatory generation of data. The classical participatory rural appraisal methods were adapted to suit local conditions, and the data revealed the needs and resources of the area, as also its strengths and weaknesses.

One of the problems faced by the village was ecological destruction caused by the practice of removing clay from paddy fields, thereby making them unfit for cultivation and rendering the water acidic due to the oozing of chemicals found in the deeper layers of the soil. This was traceable to the villagers practice of abandoning paddy cultivation on the grounds that it was not economic which had in turn, led to a number of socio-economic and environmental problems such as unemployment, scarcity of grains, vanishing of aquatic life, skin diseases and the overall destruction of bio-diversity.

The locals were persuaded that it was important to cultivate paddy fields for sustainable development, while conserving the lowlands for ecological balance. This line of thinking led to the inquiry on feasible solutions. One solution arrived at by the group was the introduction of integrated farming, a practice that had been successfully experimented with in some parts of Kuttanad in Alleppey district, Kerala, which had experienced similar problems. In this method of farming, rice is cultivated along with fish, either simultaneously or consecutively, resulting in a reduction in production costs and a corresponding increase in income. The rational behind this innovative line of thinking was to demonstrate to farmers (who had been jettisoning rice cultivation mainly because it was proving to be a losing proposition) that rice could indeed be cultivated profitably.

The local farmers, in turn, were convinced of the argument and willing to experiment with the above novel method of farming. Upon their suggestion, a team visited the experimental farms in Kuttanad and reported the findings, which were very positive. It was decided that the farming would be a group exercise, with the costs and benefits shared on an equitable basis. For further clarification and motivation, and in order to attract government support, a consultation meeting was

held, in which agricultural and fishery scientists from reputed government institutes participated. The specialists' nod of approval further
strengthened the farmers' resolve to go ahead with their experiment
with collective integrated farming. If successful, this method would
prove to be a turning point in the economy and lifestyle of the people,
as it would motivate increasing numbers of farmers to return to paddy
cultivation and produce good quality rice and fish (thereby generating
employment and income), in addition to safeguarding the local ecology
and bio-diversity.

Financial support to this programme was extended by government
departments. However, in the last planning meeting with the panchayat,
political vested interests played foul and the programme had to be
postponed. The idea is still alive, but disunity among political parties
continues to shroud it in suspense.

A Forum for Sharing and Learning

Ever since the inception of the Panchayati Raj project, Sahayi has been
conducting a series of seminars, workshops and consultation meetings,
in order to share the research findings from various stakeholders and
to create a forum for the panchayat functionaries and development
actors towards collective thinking and action. In all these programmes,
Sahayi has ensured the maximum participation of all stakeholders, with
a special emphasis on the participation of women.

A principal feature of Sahayi's seminars and workshops, greatly
appreciated by many, was their educational value. After attending a
district-level conference organised by Sahayi, the president of the
Kadakampally gram panchayat, Ms. Sathyavathy Raveendran, said:

> I loved the 'class' by Sahayi. I could share my own experiences, and also
> learnt from the practical knowledge and innovations of others. The input
> given by the Sahayi team enabled me to get a clearer understanding of the
> real situation. This will surely help me in my work.

Sathyavathy had been elected a member of the panchayat and later
became the president when her predecessor resigned after three years
in office. Since the post of the president involved several roles and

responsibilities, she had requested training by Sahayi to prepare herself for the job.

Shylaja is the secretary of the Aryanad gram panchayat. She is well versed in panchayat matters and has a reputation for functioning strictly according to the rules. This had obviously created some friction between her and the panchayat members. After attending a few of Sahayi's programmes, Shylaja confided to the Sahayi team that she had found the right group to share her difficulties with. She has since made personal visits to Sahayi to share her experiences and discuss problems, in the hope that the difficulties faced by people like her would be brought to the attention of the relevant authorities. She now acknowledges that she felt greatly relieved after sharing her experiences with the Sahayi team.

There have been other women panchayat members who had travelled from distant places to participate in the seminar on the findings of Sahayi's research study on 'Women in Panchayat'. In fact, some of these panchayat functionaries have become regular participants in Sahayi's programmes. One member even confessed to having 'never missed any of the Sahayis programmes to which I was invited.'

Building Confidence

In order to update its database in the West Kallada gram panchayat of Kollam district, where it began its micro-planning process, Sahayi mobilised a group of local women from the same panchayat to gather the socio-economic details of the households. These women were mostly housewives, who initially had their reservations about going alone to households to collect data and wished to go in threes or at least in pairs. However, after attending Sahayi's three-day training programme, which consisted of practical exercises on data generation, the women gained the confidence to carry out the survey alone. They succeeded in collecting data from more than 4,000 households in the panchayat. Sathidevi, who participated in the data collection process, said, 'This experience and Sahayi's classes have enabled us to meet many people, learn new things and develop the confidence to do social work'—a view that was shared by the rest of the group. As Chellappan, a teacher in the locality, observed, 'These women have now shown courage and interest enough to come forward and participate in the development of their own village.'

Promoting, Effective, Functioning of the Gram Sabha

The Constitution of the gram sabha has been hailed as the most dynamic element of the new Panchayati Raj legislation. The gram sabha is often described as the bulwark of democracy at the grass roots, for a vigilant gram sabha can work wonders—of which the experience of the Kottathara panchayat of Wynad district is a classic example.

On 5 June 1996, the gram sabha of Kottathara Panchayat had its first meeting, which was attended by 97 members, 27 of whom were women. A sizeable portion of the assembly also consisted of tribals. The meeting was presided over by the president of the gram panchayat, and the secretary was also present. During the meeting, one member raised the issue of the tarring of a small section (350 m) of the Karimkutty Kumbalakad Road. Several other participants joined him in requesting for details, but neither the president nor the secretary were able to provide any satisfactory answers. All they would admitt was that out of the allotted amount of Rs 1,00,000 (US$ 2,380), Rs 89,000 (US$ 2,119) had already been given to the contractor. The assembly smelled a rat because the work had only begun and there was no noticeable progress. Admittedly, there was no role for a contractor in this United Fund project, nor had the work been examined or endorsed by the engineer concerned.

The Karimkutty Kumbalakad Road boasts an intriguing history. During the period 1991–2001, as many as five contractors had siphoned off hundreds of thousands of rupees in the name of maintenance and repair works on this road. Finally, 2 km of road were tarred under the Jawahar Rozgar Yojana scheme, leaving 350 m bare. The people, who had been anxiously awaiting the completion of the work, felt badly let down by their elected leaders.

Infuriated at the authorities' sheer insensitivity and irresponsibility, the people of Kottathara decided to take matters into their own hands, and lost no time in locking up the president and the secretary in the panchayat office! They later explained that this had been done in order to prevent them from removing the files. Complaints were also registered with the higher authorities, including the district panchayat president and the district Collector, who conveniently evaded the issue until they were further pressurised. Later that evening, the officials were released after an assurance was given by the Circle Inspector of Police that the office would be guarded by the police and that action would be initiated soon.

Subsequent investigations conducted by higher officers from the block and the district confirmed the people's suspicions. Documents such as the estimate and the measurement book were not to be found. There were no entries made in the cash book after 26 April 1996, but several cheques had been issued. Though the allotted amount was only Rs 1,00,000, Rs 1,24,000 had been sanctioned, of which Rs 1,23,000 had already been paid to the contractor without any verification. The major portion of tarring work was still incomplete. This had been the manner in which previous contractors had swindled large sums of money with the connivance of panchayat authorities and officials.

The bold initiative of the Citizens' Forum (the association that was subsequently formed to address local issues) was hailed and supported by leaders of various political parties, who demanded a thorough probe into the entire episode in order to expose the culprits and bring them to book. The Citizens' Forum also submitted a petition to the Minister for Local Administration. The state vigilance machinery was set in motion gradually but, it was hoped, more resolutely than during previous times.

Nevertheless, it was gratifying to note that among the leaders of the gram sabha mentioned above were persons trained by Sahayi.

Policy Advocacy

Research is an integral part of Sahayi's Panchayati Raj activities, and special attention is paid to ensure that research is conducted in a participatory manner. In all our research studies, the data-generation process has been a mutual learning experience for both Sahayi and the participants. In studies such as 'Panchayat Finances: A case study of Kerala', the research team discovered that some panchayats had not prepared their annual financial statements for over two years. The panchayat functionaries later said that the visits and presence of the research team had motivated them to prepare their annual statements of accounts, and in one panchayat, the research team had actually helped prepare the account books. There were also several instances where the respondents had asked the team for clarifications and relevant information, which underscores their need for capacity-building.

During the preparation of a draft report of a study, the preliminary findings are shared with a select group of stakeholders to elicit their opinions and suggestions. The final draft is shared with a representative group of stakeholders from the state, including the concerned minister, politicians, bureaucrats, panchayat functionaries, leaders of voluntary organisations and the media. For effective policy lobbying, the final report is circulated among policy-makers, including ministers.

One of the major issues highlighted by the Panchayat finances study was the spillover effect observed in the expenditure of the Jawahar Rozgar Yojana (JRY) funds. This was also reflected in a circular issued by the Rural Development (PB) Department (No.1426/ PB1/ 99/ RDD) dated 5 February 1999, which stated that unless the local bodies took the initiative to accelerate the momentum of implementation of JRY funds, a proportionate cut would have to be made in the amount given by the Government of India, in order to compensate for the shortfall in expenditure.

Another point raised in the case study concerned the need for self-financing (to the extent possible) by the panchayats and the maximum utilisation of these funds within the stipulated time. This was reflected in the criteria adopted subsequently by the local administration department for the selection of the 'best panchayat'.

Another concern expressed in the same study concerned the low performance levels of women PRI members, who often had to play multiple and concurrent roles of teacher, housewife and PRI member/president. To this end, the government executed a policy decision that henceforth, school or college teachers taking up the position of president would have to take long leave while in office.

Community-Level Changes

We have briefly mentioned the positive impact of Sahayi's capacity-building innovations on individuals and groups, which often spill over to the communities surrounding them, thereby creating ripple effects of empowerment among the people. Take, for example, the case of Hindu Dalits and Christian Dalits—two groups at loggerheads on the issue of reservation to Dalit converts to Christianity. This disunity had damaging effects on the efforts of movements like the Dalit Panthers to build up Dalit solidarity in order to address common issues. To reduce misunderstanding and promote unity, in 1997, the Dalit Panthers launched an all-Kerala unity campaign under the leadership of Ambujakshan and his team. Drawing inspiration from the philosophy of participation, and strengthened by the new insights and skills they had gained from Sahayi's capacity-building programmes, they worked out an effective strategy. After the campaign, several rival organisations were dismantled, and people began to co-operate, regardless of their religious affiliations.

In some SHGs, such as the Aiswarya Vanitha Group in Thuravoor, women have introduced the innovative practice of pooling savings in kind rather in cash when they are short of funds. This ensures that some saving is made every day, even if it is just a handful of rice. These savings are pooled and made available to needy women on a loan basis every week. This is seen as an effective way of addressing the problem of poverty. Radhamoni, a member of the SHG, said that they got this idea and inspiration from Sahayi's training.

Positive changes were reported in the attitude and extent of co-operation from women SHGs in Kuttanad, as a result of the change in their female leaders' attitudes and behaviour. As Annamma Joseph of the St. Joseph Group, Pallikkotuma, Kuttanad observed:

> Earlier, she (the president) was a dictator and very tough and non-cooperative so we were reluctant to attend the meetings and participate in

the discussions. But after the training she has become very understanding; she listens to us. We love to attend meetings and participate in the process of taking decisions and implementing them. Now we feel that this is our own organisation, for improving our conditions.

Elsamma Devasya of the same SHG pointed out how changes in the SHG were reflected in their families. When husbands and children observed positive changes in the women, they became very appreciative of the SHG movement and encouraged them to attend meetings. Said a proud Elsamma:

Initially my husband warned me not to cooperate with the SHGs and my children discouraged me from participating in the meetings and other activities of the SHGs, but after observing the positive changes in me, they are now encouraging me to take part in the activities, reminding me about the meeting. If the meeting is conducted late in the evening, my husband accompanies me there.

There are also stories of women bonding together and effectively resisting administrative malpractice. For instance, in Athani in the district of Ernakulam, women joined together to form a pressure group in the panchayat. Today they keenly watch and monitor events in the panchayat and bring any wrongdoing, malpractice or injustice that comes to their notice to the attention of superior authorities. The panchayat is therefore doubly cautious.

The members of the Anaswara Mahila Samajam, also at Athani, successfully manage a garment-making unit with funds from the Khadi and Village Industries Commission, which employs several women. The leader of the organisation has made full use of the knowledge and skill acquired from Sahayi's training and, as one of the 'beneficiaries' said, 'This has helped me work and earn, enhanced the family income and improved my status.'

Lathika Bai is the standing committee chairperson of the Sasthamcotta gram panchayat, who attended Sahayi's training on microplanning. In fact, the resource-mapping exercise was done in front of her house. After the training she confided to a friend, 'Now I know the resources of my ward. Previously I had no idea.' The training boosted her confidence and she began to involve herself more seriously in the affairs of the panchayat. The newly-gained knowledge about the resources of her ward helped her to formulate a plan for a drinking water project for the village. She identified for the first time the areas where water was available in her ward. An overhead tank would be constructed atop a nearby hill and water would soon be made available to all the families. Were it not for Sahayi's capacity-building intervention, this simple problem-solving exercise would not have happened.

The small Dalit community of Ambalavayal, Wynad, solved its drinking-water problem in a different way. When their appeals to the panchayat and government authorities for assistance met with indifference, the people of Ambalavayal decided to act on their own. With the support of Arshabharath, a voluntary organisation that had been trained by Sahayi, they conducted several rounds of participatory microplanning. This process empowered the community, which decided to construct a well and an elevated overhead tank for easy distribution to all the households. Land and labour were provided by the people, who also raised supplementary resources. After a year's community deliberations, contribution, and hard work, the community drinking-water project was finally completed. The participatory approach and involvement of Arshabharath helped motivate the people into collective action to solve their problem themselves.

PART III: SAHAYI'S CONSTRAINTS

Sahayi has remained a small organisation—its senior staff number less than ten—with a core group of facilitators, resource persons and research staff. Sahayi does not have a training centre of its own, and the turnover of senior staff has been a major constraint. Primarily, this has been due to lack of resources to offer moderate compensation packages to competent professionals, as Kerala is no longer a priority area for major funding agencies. Further, capacity-building programmes seldom find a place in the agenda of leading international donor agencies. Sahayi initially received programme support from a few agencies, such as the Institute of International Cooperation of the German Adult Education Association (IIZ/DVV), Germany; CEBEMO, Netherlands; and PRIA, New Delhi. Some of the international partner organisations which initially supported the programmes have practically left the scene, so Sahayi receives continuous support only from IIZ/DVV and PRIA.

The strategy of generating income from training programmes has not been successful. The need for professionalism in managing NGOs is yet to be realised by the leading ones. In popular perception, social workers serving the NGO and VDO sector should give their services for free. The sector therefore cannot attract professionals, who expect to be paid for their services. As capacity building is a low priority on the small and medium NGO and VDO agenda, they do not have the capacity to pay adequate salaries; so paid training programmes receive a low response.

To some extent, Sahayi has been able to change the perspective and culture of these organisations and make them realise the need for capacity-building. Some of these organisations do pay for training services. The top leaders of the relatively large NGOs and VDOs initially kept away from the programmes of Sahayi. To sell the idea of capacity-building to the leaders of large NGOs, perspective building seminars were organised involving NGO and VDO leaders who were initially negative or apathetic towards Sahayi. The attitude has started slowly changing.

The state government runs a broad scheme for training elected people's representatives of the *Panchayati Raj* institutions, but the impact of such traditional training is being questioned. Despite the fact that the top officials of the state administration fully appreciate the capabilities of Sahayi, they do not sponsor officials or elected leaders of the local self-governance institutions to attend Sahayi's programmes. This is primarily because Sahayi does not have an adequate training infrastructure.

During its initial years, Sahayi was not strict about selecting participants for the training programmes, relying completely on the nominations received from the NGOs. From our follow-up observations, we found that participants who work at the lower level generally could not make use of the inputs received. One major reason for this was a lack of support from organisation leaders to use the new skills acquired by lower-level staff. To overcome this, Sahayi established a rapport with organisational leaders and involved them in some perspective-building programmes. However, several small organisations were not able to utilise the inputs received due to lack of resources. Realising this waste of effort, Sahayi subsequently became more selective in respect to participants and participating organisations and developed a clear set of selection criteria which are strictly adhered to now.

The greatest constraint faced by Sahayi, today, is that it is not able to fully meet the demand for capacity-building training and interventions. Its infrastructural limitations and 'resource crunch' are fundamental problems. Sahayi has received financial support in the form of short-term project funds from some agencies. However, there is hardly any financial support for long-term involvement. Uncertainty about resource availability is a major constraint for implementing a perspective plan.

PART IV: PROJECT FINDINGS

Each capacity-building intervention has been a learning experience for Sahayi. We shall list some of the key discoveries:

- Empowerment is a complex, organic, personal or group process. It presupposes several physical conditions, but is not a mechanical process. Rather, it is a highly personal process. It touches the inner recesses of cognition, perception and emotion of the individual involved. The individual's intelligence and freedom must be respected and nurtured in a non-threatening atmosphere. This calls for a high degree of integration, authenticity and resourcefulness on the part of the facilitators.

- Empowerment through capacity building requires an integrated, holistic approach. It also demands sustained efforts from all the actors in the process. It begins with the trainee or participant, who must have the proper motivation and readiness to undergo the transformation process. This has to be kept in mind during the trainee-selection period.

- It is important to build up and maintain a creative climate of participation from the very first stage of planning to the end of the process. Involving the participants in every stage and winning their confidence has been found to be highly effective.

- The empowerment process, particularly in modern times, demands a constructive blend of humanism and professionalism. Humanism is the background to understanding and empathetic support, while professionalism is the technical know-how and application. These two elements have to work in unison. They are sometimes divorced from each other and therefore the goal of empowerment is not attained. What is needed is a judicious blend of the two.

• Empowerment is the result of individual and group self-discovery about their innate goodness and creativity. One insight will lead to a form of self-expression, which in turn generates further insight. The process is one of continuous de-education and re-education; of learning, unlearning, and re-learning. Perceptions and perspectives are constantly challenged and revised on the basis of experienced reality. Articulating the newly gained insights makes participants clear and focused, and this clarity of vision leads to genuine and appropriate action, in which empowerment comes to fruition. It is important to ensure that this process is not interrupted either by internal disturbances or external interference. This is the role of the facilitator.

• Capacity-building interventions need to be suitably followed up and strengthened with additional and ongoing inputs. This is essential for ensuring the natural growth of the process and its consequences. During training, only the seed is sown. It has to germinate and grow to produce its expected fruits. For this, a favourable climate must be in place in the arena where the trainees will practice what they have learnt. Where the leaders of the NGOs and VDOs were very supportive, the impact has been pronounced. Where support has been lacking, the results have been minimal or absent. Therefore, it is important that the facilitators maintain rapport not only with the trainees, but also with the leaders or chief functionaries of the respective organisations. Sahayi has been insistent on this subject. A related point is that those who complete training should have the opportunity to practice what they have learnt.

• Building up a receptive external socio-political environment is an essential condition for the free, full practice of the findings. To address this, Sahayi plans policy advocacy interventions and meetings between different actors.

• Participatory methods are most effective in empowering marginalised sections of society. Initially there may be some resistance, since they may have developed defense mechanisms as a result of their experience of prolonged suppression. But one has to be patient with these individuals or groups, and

once the ice is broken, they will accept the new method with
great enthusiasm.

- The empowering process has been found to be very effective among women, whose innate tendencies are participatory,
but which have been repressed by the dominant male ethos.
The spark of self-confidence generated during the capacity-
building experience continues to grow, generating energies for
participatory action.

- Participatory methods of empowerment have tremendous
scope in the new local self-governance institutions of the panchayats and nagarpalikas. The functioning of gram sabhas/ward
councils could also be dramatically improved if the proceedings are facilitated in a participatory manner. This would lead
to the slow transformation of the village communities along
equitable and sustainable lines. The response of PRI members
to participatory methods has been very positive. Extending the
participatory approaches to the panchayat will have far-reaching
effects.

- Our experiments in microplanning have generated a number
of discoveries, of which the most important is that local people,
if given some guidance, are capable of identifying and analysing
their problems and working out collective solutions. A corollary
to this is that the facilitators have to be extremely sensitive to
local conditions and adapt the methods of participatory planning processes accordingly. A second discovery is that blind
politics is the bane of development and a handful of venomous
elements can sabotage a good proposal by the majority. Over-
politicisation has been pointed out as the biggest stumbling
block against sustainable development of the state.

- Those in power—the entrenched political parties and other
interested groups—will do everything to neutralise empowering participatory processes. One therefore has to be vigilant and
find ways of mitigating the negative influences and overcoming
obstacles.

CONCLUSION

The ground covered by Sahayi in the empowerment of the CSO leaders and their target groups through capacity-building interventions is

significant, especially considering the limited resources at its command. However, we have only scratched at the surface of the issue. The scope and need for work in this area is tremendous. It is becoming increasingly clear to every reflective individual in the development sector that only through the introduction of holistic methods can we hope to extricate ourselves from the mesh of problems in which we are caught. The future undoubtedly belongs to capacity building through participatory approaches. Sahayi is committed to the pursuit of its goal of facilitating this process, leading to the empowerment of the weakest sections of society and thereby heralding the advent of a just, equitable, gender-sensitive and environment-friendly society.

In conclusion, I shall cite the views of Adv. M. P. Varkey (retired Deputy Director of Panchayats in Kerala, and an authority on self-governance institutions) and Dr Hanno Schindele, Programme Officer, Institute for International Co-operation of the German Adult Education Association (IIZ/DVV), Germany.

The development contribution of Sahayi has been that it has prepared the voluntary organisations to work for rural development, mainly through capacity building. The great thing about Sahayi is that it has made maximum use of its resources. With scarce resources, Sahayi has achieved marvellous results.

I must point out that Sahayi is the only voluntary agency engaged in research or study in the Panchayati Raj area. Its studies are objective — they bring out the actual facts without distorting them to serve partisan ends. The findings of Sahayi's studies have helped the functionaries, like the secretaries, to engage in introspection. The studies have also brought the issues before the government, the media, etc.

An important strength of Sahayi is that it uses methods which are intelligible and useful to the common man. It is free from prejudice and operates with an open mind, maintaining a secular and scientific temper (Adv. M.P. Varkey).

Sahayi and the other IIZ/DVV partners are particularly stressing the participation of the discriminated, impoverished people in the local self-governance institutions through awareness raising and training .... Through increasingly successful advocacy activities, regional support organisations like Sahayi are contributing to the reinforcement of the basic human rights of the underprivileged, often against strong opposition from the elites. It can be stated that Sahayi and the other Indian Partners of IIZ/DVV are reaching their objective of empowerment and capacity building of the poorest sections of society to an increasing extent, and they are gaining growing respect and acknowledgement in their respective areas (Dr Hanno Schindele).

REFERENCE

PRIA (1991), *Voluntary Development Organisations in India: A Study of History, Roles and Future Challenges*. New Delhi: PRIA.

Conclusion

Mukul Sharma

What is empowerment? Is it hegemony and control of one over another as a new manifestation of power? Does it imply development and providing people a baseline security of lives and livelihood? Is it about acquiring the awareness and skills necessary to take charge of one's own life chances and about facilitating the ability of individuals and groups to make their own decisions? Does it indicate taking a stand against the politics of disempowerment? Is it a process of conscientisation and being involved in decision-making processes? Does it signify the gaining of power by the oppressed? Does it hold some distinct connotation for women's organisations? And finally, does it mean all this and more?

It was during the third and final day of the first residency in September 1999 in New Delhi that all the contributors to this volume got involved in a discussion about the meaning of this much-used word. Pertinent questions had been raised regarding the presentation of their research proposals over the previous two days. For instance, the six Rural Support Programmes in Pakistan cover half of the country's 112 districts, and are seen as the biggest actors in rural development, next only to the government. Do the largeness of scale and financial resources offer space for the strengthening of the organisation of the empowered communities, and will it last even if the currently supportive governments and donor agencies decided to turn their backs on it? To take another example, Sahayi is a support organisation of NGOs in South India whose capacity-building programme is said to be qualitative rather than quantitative. However, how does one measure the qualitative and ensure that a new hierarchy does not emerge among the NGOs? Also, while women may have received support from the Women's Centre for Change, Penang, to what extent has it empowered them as well? Similarly, in Sri Lanka, Satyodaya works with extremely poor estate workers, but how far can an outside agency bring about conscientisation among the marginalised and the excluded?

Sifting through these and other questions, a listing of certain 'indicators' of empowerment was made, which included popular consciousness about problems, the ability to articulate and influence policy and decision-making outside of one's group, the existence of people's organisations, emergence of leaders and activists, increased literacy and income, enhanced mobility, competency and efficiency, self-reliance, control and management of resources, sustainability, etc. Such a list of indicators further enriched our understanding of the term 'empowerment'. While the experiences of the four NGOs have revealed how such an understanding influences their work, the nature of their organisations and the range of their activities, the understanding of the meaning of the word 'empowerment', in turn, suggests useful insights that can enlarge or challenge existing explanations of power and powerlessness.

POWER, POWERLESSNESS AND EMPOWERMENT

Empowerment does not take place in a social vacuum. Powerlessness is brought about through a historical process, which leads to a denial and violation of even the basic rights of life and livelihood, and causes subjugation, which in turn reinforces the entire process. Empowerment thus becomes an essential tool for the destitute, the hungry and the vulnerable, in order to solve their problems. To be empowered means at least three things. At a personal level, it means developing a sense of self-confidence and capacity, and undoing the effects of internalised oppression. At a relational level, it means developing the ability to negotiate and influence the nature of a relationship and decisions made within it. And at a collective level, it means coming together for collective action, to achieve better results for a wider group of people.

However, empowerment, rather than merely occurring on the ruins of the power system also has to work within it. Power can be manifest in diverse ways, both positive and negative. The most common understanding of power has been of 'power over', i.e. the ability of one person or group to get another person or group to do something against their will. It can also be manifest in the shaping of people's perceptions, cognitions and preferences, so that they accept their role in the existing order of things. It can manifest itself in the predominance of men over other men or of men over women. It can also be illusive, something which can be given by one person to another, and just as easily withdrawn. Joanna Rowlands, in her landmark study, describes other ways of understanding and conceptualising power. They can be described as 'power to', 'power with' and 'power from within'—all of which allow the construction of different meanings for 'empowerment'[1]. 'Power to' involves gaining access to a full range of human abilities and potential, to have a say in decisions, to take pride in one's own ability. It can be generative and productive, creating new possibilities and actions without domination. 'Power with' is the capacity to achieve with others what one could not have achieved alone, and a sense of the whole as being greater than the sum of the individuals, especially when a group tackles the problems together. 'Power from within' is self-generated and arises from a recognition that one is neither helpless nor the source of all one's problems, and that one is, in fact, restricted in part by structures outside oneself. Its basis is self-acceptance and self-respect, which, in turn, extends to respect for and acceptance of others as equals. All these are central to empowerment, and the NGOs in this book have been working towards them in various capacities.

The experience of NGOs in Asia reveals that the everyday lives of people within the new order are being shaped by constant tensions between the old and the new. The long days of colonialism and domination of various kinds, from within and without, and of still being a part of the periphery in the new emerging globalised world, makes power naturalised in forms of life, and habitualised and internalised in segments of our societies. Consciousness of power, and the capacity to recognise it and contest it, is what differentiates liberating empowerment from hegemonic power. Power and empowerment are not polar opposites here. What matter are the concrete social, political and cultural conditions and actions that transform dominating, centralised power into shareable, contestable power.

In addition, power is never total. Powerlessness is always partial. Power remains vulnerable to that which it excludes. The vitality and resistance of the forms of life it thwarts or impedes, offer a space for the powerless to acquire their own influence. This is a pull factor, on which individuals and groups come together, and try to change the potential they possess.

For the Rural Support Programmes of Pakistan, the imparting to the poor of a new power is a goal in itself and 'constructing a group identity, raising consciousness, acquiring new skills, upgrading the knowledge base of the poor' are the means for it. For Sahayi in India, the creation of a just, participatory and self-sustainable society comes 'only through equitable interaction and re-distribution of power among the various constituents of society'. In addition, its emphasis on local self-governance institutions, such as panchayats in villages and nagarpalikas in towns, is located in the realm of power. Training, education and mobilisation of people and elected representatives is exclusively directed to claim their share of power, and exercise it effectively. The Women's

Centre for Change, of Penang emphasises the strategy of 'managing' and 'sharing' power for the growth of the organisation and the individual. In Sri Lanka, Satyodaya has realised the limitations of the role of an outside agency or an NGO, and wills the plantation workers to empower themselves directly as much as possible.

Extreme environmental conditions, remote geographical locations, rudimentary physical and social infrastructure, underdeveloped markets and inadequate investment in financial and human capital in rural Pakistan have not deterred the poor from responding positively to the rural development programmes. They are not forlorn, pessimistic or uncertain. The diary of an organiser captures this: 'When I reached the place, within 15 minutes, 30 women had gathered'. Training and awareness programmes of Sahayi in India have led to remarkable changes in the lives of many people who run various other NGOs. Similarly, in Sri Lanka and Malaysia, where communities nurse deep-rooted prejudices against and tensions between each other along religious or ethnic lines, efforts for peace and justice based on arguments for heterogeneity in a plural society have instantly shown rays of hope.

DEVELOPMENT YARDSTICKS

Many critics of present day development tend to romanticise 'village', 'pre-modern', 'community' consciousness and 'traditional' wisdom, and take a totally anti-development stance. There is a rejection of modernity and an endorsement of all that is traditional. However, debate within such polarised categories is, intellectually and for practical purposes, not very useful. On the other hand, ever since trade unions, social organisations and peoples' movements have attempted to address the development problems in post-colonial Asia, a principal tool has been to organise the unorganised, the poor and the marginalised, and to agitate, often against the state, for a better world.

The NGOs in India, Pakistan, Malaysia and Sri Lanka described in this volume have tried to develop their own indices of development in their respective fields of operation. These range from the meeting of basic needs to a more general improvement of the quality of life. There is no single goal of socio-economic development, just as there is no sure guidance on the choice of measures and their relative weights.

The range and complexity of the needs being addressed by the four organisations varies immensely. When Satyodaya started its work among the Tamil plantation workers in Sri Lanka, it had to meet two basic objectives simultaneously: first, to take up developmental work, so that needs such as food, water, and education could be met, and second, work to ease the ethnic and communal tension in the area. Thus, Satyodaya began with base-level developmental work, and soon established community centres and libraries to bring the Sinhala villagers and the Tamil estate workers together. The provision of emotional, legal and direct services, through trained volunteers and staff, to the victims and survivors of violence was part and parcel of the Women's Centre for Change, Penang since its inception. For the Rural Support Programmes in Pakistan, the most pressing need was to address the problems of rural poverty and underdevelopment. To achieve this, they evolved a number of programmes—from natural resource management to rural credit, addressing gender issues, creating a physical infrastructure, and providing for basic needs such as shelter and education. Sahayi in India had to ensure proper training and information dissemination to the NGOs, and it began this process with the smaller organisations that had the least infrastructure.

These studies signify that NGOs play crucial roles—although they may take diverse forms—in ensuring that development signifies economic security for all, providing basic services to everyone, ensuring the maximum participation of people in every level of decision-making, and achieving democratisation of everyday life.

SOCIAL JUSTICE

Where there is fulfilment of basic needs, there is the possibility of social justice. But in societies characterised by deep-rooted discrimination on the basis of caste, gender or ethnicity, social justice also means that groups such as ethnic minorities, rural people and women will be free from the burden of injustice. Thus, while meeting their basic needs, the approach here has to address other needs and issues as well.

This is a very loosely defined area encompassing a whole range of human, social, cultural and political factors. Thus, when the focus is on the alleviation of rural poverty through a variety of measures in Pakistan, attention to what is being produced is supported by attention to how much is being produced, how, for whom, and with what impact and future. When the work is concentrated on the strengthening of democracy and democratic institutions in India, the idea of democracy extends beyond the existence of formal mechanisms to include a stress on grass-roots institutions, people's participation, access to the governmental decision-making processes, and effective channels of accountability for public officials. When the work is focused on an ethnic minority in Sri Lanka, there is also an aim to strengthen a plural society and to eliminate unjust divisions within it. Tackling violence against women in Malaysia also means addressing prevailing social values and structures. The social factors addressed by the projects are wide and include equality, participation, peace, justice and sustainability. All, however, present difficult problems of measurement when it comes to gauging impact.

All this needs to be perceived within a broader conceptual framework. While the work of the Women's Centre for Change, Penang does not give us much of an idea about the kind of political society and democratic space to which they aspire, we can derive some broad hints from it, as it is concerned not only with the relief and rehabilitation of women victims, but also with the ultimate end of ensuring a just, equal and violence-free life for them. This end could well be applied to the whole of society.

While these social indicators are difficult to measure, both immediately and over the long run, they do provide a long-term vision. They go beyond measuring development only in terms of literacy, access to water, calorific consumption, life expectancy and so on. They also point to common and shared values and problems, to alternative ways of development in Asia. There seems to be a clear need in Asia to develop specific social purposes related to the poor, to see their relationship with broader democratic goals, and work for them.

EMPOWERMENT AS A WOMEN'S ISSUE

The goal of women's empowerment is not just to change hierarchical gender relations but to change all hierarchical relations in society—class, caste, race, ethnic and North–South relations. Women are an essential concern of many Asian NGOs. When talking of women, they mean their socially constructed and culturally determined position, the assumptions made about their skills and abilities, the conditions in which they live and work, the relations that exist between women and men. They include social relations, and relations of power and control based on gender. This is evident from the description of those programmes that have been developed to bring about changes in women's positions and to shift the balance of power and control towards greater parity between women and men.

In Pakistan, Sri Lanka and, to some extent, in India, there is the challenge to provide basic opportunities for poor women, for whom poverty becomes the basis of discrimination and disadvantage. Rural poor women in Pakistan and Sri Lanka are handicapped in many ways, particularly by limited access to land and related resources, lack of control over their own labour and the fruits of their labour, lack of mobility due to social and cultural restrictions, as well as the burden of responsibility borne for family survival and subsistence. Thus, developmental and income-generation programmes have become the major points of focus where gender concerns have been articulated over the last decade. The Rural Support Programmes amongst rural women took up self-employment, training for small-scale enterprise promotion, vegetable cultivation and marketing credit, in a big way. Similarly, the rural women in Sri Lanka were trained in animal husbandry, sewing and commercial flower cultivation, and are now actively involved in them. Sahayi, even while focusing on its main task of capacity-building for women's organisations, has also assisted women's self-help groups involved in thrift and credit programmes.

These programmes have also demonstrated that a change in women's positions is not merely concerned with a restructuring of their economic lives, but that it has to go much beyond. It also depends on changes in social and organisational structures, systems, relations and values which constrain and restrain women. There is a need for new initiatives, which draw attention to the different levels at which actions are needed. There are at least three such levels at which these NGOs have worked. The first is the symbolic level, where strong signals can be sent about what is important and valued in the organisation. When Sahayi adopted the capacity-building programme for women's organisations and self-help groups as one of its priority programmes, and Satyodaya characterised its women's programmes as 'special programmes', they sent messages across to all their members, partner organisations and other NGOs. Beneath this level are the levels of organisational practice and values. Thus we see Satyodaya constituting a committee of 30 women, and each of these women, in turn, organising women's committees in their own areas. We also see women becoming an increasingly essential part of community organisations by Sahayi in India, which focuses on skills and values for women's empowerment.

Thus, income-generation and other specific activities can at best be seen as a process, rather than a product, for women's empowerment. Thereafter, other levels of action will follow, as action at any one level alone is unlikely to be effective, and may lead to a gap between rhetoric and action. Action at the symbolic level (such as renaming or adapting a programme or putting women leaders at the local level) can never be effective unless it is linked to the creation of new overall systems and structures, and gender-sensitive training (such as perspective-building orientation, leadership development, courses in self-group management, consultancy and counselling), which, in turn, will only be effective if they are part of a much broader strategy for organisational change.

There is also a need to move beyond the project and programme work of NGOs into the realm of policy making. Naila Kabeer has written of 'the disempowering and infantilizing ways in which policy makers have frequently treated the poor, particularly poor women'[2], and she is of the view that the long-term sustainability of empowerment strategies will depend on the extent to which the policy makers envision women struggling within a given set of policy priorities and the extent to which they empower them to challenge and reverse these priorities. It is only when the participation of poorer women goes beyond participation at the project level, to intervening in the broader policy-making agenda that their strategic interests can become an enduring influence on the course of development. For the overall empowerment of women, it is the mind-set of the policy makers, bureaucrats and of the women concerned that would have to be changed.

Among these case studies, the Women's Centre for Change, Penang has particularly shown the ability and the strength of the NGO to not only provide support to women, but equally importantly, to step up pressure on the government and policy makers to pass a crucial Act. Similarly, village women of Kerala in India, associated with Sahayi's programmes, have revealed a change in their mind-sets, as they are beginning to actively engage with wider issues of local self-planning and governance at the panchayat level.

ON ORGANISATION, PARTICIPATION AND CONSCIENTISATION

Organisation, participation and conscientisation are interlinked concepts and their stories in NGOs may unfold in various ways. The usual approach is linear, chronological, beginning when the idea of an organisation has taken root and how a particular organisational form has then evolved through efforts to implement programmes. This is the narrative of the Rural Support Programmes in Pakistan. The participation of the rural poor in planning, managing, financing and extending programmes has been assured and sustained through the broad-based community organisations. The leadership role has been taken over by the rural people themselves, as their efforts, ideas and commitments are mobilised.

A different story emerges from Sri Lanka, where Fr. Caspersz, as the founder co-ordinator of Satyodaya, played a decisive role in all its activities for 25 years and under whose able stewardship the organisation evolved and grew from strength to strength. The success of Satyodaya as an organisation suggests that one ought not to be deterred when an aura of personal greatness is associated with the leadership of an organisation. This also indicates that the one-person leadership style is still largely operative in some NGOs.

In many ways, NGOs are concerned with creating futures, by envisioning desired states and designing structures to bring them about. The end goal gives shape and meaning to a particular form of organisation. Simultaneously, 'contemporary' thoughts, feelings and associations also motivate and give reason to organisations. The Women's Centre for Change, Penang, began with a deep sense of voluntarism and togetherness among a core group of activists. They wanted their organisation to be free from the power struggle and the domination of particular individuals or groups. Towards this goal, they decided to rotate their general committee periodically. Sahayi evolved its training programme with goals like democratic control, shared collective leadership, co-operation and teamwork in mind. Sometimes, problematic experiences motivate NGOs to reorganise, and these experiences may give new or wider meaning to organisations. A divide within the Women's Centre for Change in 1993 made the organisation more vigilant, by creating a degree of ethnic balance in its Committee.

The experiences here suggest that NGOs can achieve participation at micro levels of activity in diverse and innovative ways. The modes and extent of participation may vary across types of activities, but involve striking a balance between the pursuit of efficient ways of management and the principles of equality and justice.

However, participation is merely the first step. It has to be followed by a concrete process of conscientisation. But the language of participation and conscientisation can all too easily turn into rhetoric and be used as 'buzzwords' by some organisations to achieve their objectives. Planners frequently use this rhetoric to justify decisions already taken. Paulo Freire's concept of conscientisation, the idea that the poor need to develop a critical awareness of their own society in order to take more command over their own lives, has been widely accepted as a true definition of the word.[3] It signifies their learning about and understanding of situations that may at times seem complex and difficult, but which they know they have the ability to grasp. It implies a liberation of the poor through a new awareness. Strategies aimed at conscientisation are crucial to the struggle against oppression.

At a functional level, it means that people must be consulted at every stage to achieve a true participatory process. Conscientisation further involves a more complex process of commitment by an NGO to allow the pace and character of change to be determined by the local people, to support their capacity to analyse the constraints and opportunities they face and to facilitate access to the resources needed for improvement of their conditions. The scope of involvement here is much wider than that of functional forms of participation as it implies a willingness to be led by the wishes of a community or a group of people. It is therefore not enough to have just a contractual relationship between NGOs and the people, but essentially involves two-way consultation, collaboration and equal interaction.

NGO functioning, like other aspects of human experience, is quite complicated. Glimpses of problems mentioned in the Indian, Malaysian and Sri Lankan case studies show that NGOs are grappling with broader issues of institutional functioning. The problem of reliance on one person may motivate them to search for a more participative and decentralised structure. More often than not, this type of structure helps organisations to define the problem of unequal ethnic and gender participation. NGOs today have evolved at many interacting levels. At the level of their own association, the evolution concerns activism, leadership, entrepreneurship, vision and goals. At that of their work, it may concern activism and its dynamics, demands and aspirations. At that of relationships, it will be about the public institutions of government, political parties and support networks. A robust organisational structure depends on an appropriate democratic environment and an equal partnership with support networks. Indeed, the development of democratic public institutions is predicated on the strengthening of viable democratic organisations. There is often tension and disharmony between these many levels—sometimes NGOs lag behind because their legal–political structures do not match their purposes, or because the sheer pace of their work makes their structures inadequate.

In these case studies, the main focus has been on what the NGOs and their target populations are doing at the micro level. But at the same time, it is also clear that the NGOs evolve into broader-based programmes and, occasionally, into social forces, enabling them to enter into spheres of action and decision on surrounding issues. How far micro leads to macro; how far 'action' has percolated down to everyday lives; how far the NGOs themselves will resist becoming complacent or co-opted; how far they will be able to sustain themselves as an empowering force—all these are yet to be tested.

POLITICAL DECENTRALISATION

The theme of state decentralisation has found takers among NGOs. Every act of decentralisation, after all, implies a redistribution of power. This gives it a pre-eminently political context, which not only includes institutional and normative aspects, but also other complex issues such as the transformation of the behaviour of individuals (people, politicians, elected representatives and citizens) and of political culture in general. When we speak of decentralisation, we inevitably imply a new way of 'making politics', which demands a process of acceptance of new values and social pedagogy.

Recent constitutional amendments in India gave local self-governance institutions, such as panchayats and nagarpalikas, power and resources. Through these amendments it was hoped that the important aims of democratisation, and the finding of solutions to problems related to the meeting of basic needs, would be accomplished. Strengthening local powers can bring decisions closer to citizens, allow for greater fulfilment of citizens' needs and aspirations, improve the efficiency of information and personal services, and achieve greater citizen participation in local management. There are, however, many problems, as revealed in the case study from India. The people are not enlightened and united enough to effectively demand their share of power; there is over-politicisation of local governance and a resistance to change on the part of politicians and bureaucrats; a lack of required perspectives or competence among elected representatives; and a considerable degree of passivity among citizens.

Sahayi has evolved a multidimensional strategy, involving programmes of awareness generation, skill development, policy research, consultancy, information dissemination, publication and networking. It is neither polemical nor narrowly parochial. Here, the building of a participatory democracy has been conceived as a combination of forms of management development and grass-roots democracy, involving voting, elections, campaigns, meetings, training, micro-planning, and local resource persons. It strives to give confidence and a sense of participatory political culture to those who have long been socially and culturally powerless.

This is about gaining and strengthening political power at the base, through which decisions, particularly those that affect people's day-to-day living, will be made. Political power is not only the power to vote but also the power of voice and of collective action. There could be immense possibilities for this power.

But despite the successful establishment of decentralisation and local self-governance in some quarters of India, central and state governments still retain the core of political power. While experiments with grass-roots democracy are thus important, they are only a partial means of achieving a meaningful democratisation of the political system and society as a whole. Without a clear reference to the state, local institutions can regress into a morass of self-management of only minor activities, which could well be lost within the mainstream political current. Thus, the relationship of NGOs with governments, even when problematic, becomes an important agenda for debate.

NEGOTIATING WITH THE STATE

It has been observed that development does not take place on the basis of projects which will 'remain irrelevant to the majority of the needy unless used as beacons to light up pathways for others—notably the state— to pursue. Popular participation on a significant scale will only come about through reforms in official structures, not through multiplying NGO projects.'[4] NGOs' actions and their relations with the state are determined to a large extent by the political, economic and cultural context in which they operate. The particular political conditions and bureaucratic procedures of government authorities experienced by an NGO, control many of the opportunities of NGO activity, and set very specific parameters to the extent to which NGOs participate in different provisions.

Few development interventions undertaken by NGOs are politically neutral. However, the relationship between NGOs and the state is not a tidy one, and is filled with ambiguities, ranging from the conflictive to the collaborative. On the one hand, there is the danger that the state might forget its own responsibilities towards the people and leave it to NGOs to fulfil its role. NGOs can never take over the role of the state in providing infrastructure and services to the poor. It has also been rightly pointed out that 'the distinctive role of the voluntary sector is not to serve as a cheap contractor to implement government-defined programmes.'[5] Moreover, it is often seen that there is limited commitment to the aforementioned relationship on the part of the state, so that the burden of making it work falls disproportionately heavily on the NGOs. The most problematic of course is the fact that the state interests may often remain linked to those of the elite and dominant in society, thus putting the state and the NGO in a conflictive mode. There may be a marked difference in visions and models of development pursued by each side. The NGOs may see the state as bureaucratic, corrupt and totally unsympathetic to the needs of the poor and thus wish to completely avoid it, as it puts their credibility at risk. The state may also think that NGO mobilisation work could promote social instability, that it could weaken government mandate and credibility, and could well increase the demand for government services beyond its capacity to meet it.

On the other hand however, with the steady increase in activities of NGOs, the need for institutionalised means of communication between NGOs and the state has become all the more urgent. From this relationship, the state stands to gain access to a better network of distribution, a higher quality of contact with sections of the population that it has failed to reach out to, more information from the grass roots, and enhanced cost effectiveness. NGOs' experience in developing and implementing participatory methods can serve as material from which government services could learn and 'scale up' innovations developed by NGOs. The NGO stands to benefit from access to policy formulation, access to skills, facilities and technologies of government agencies/departments, and above all the greater resources available through the government. It is an unquestionable fact the state is a major player and that without its collaboration, the lot of the poor cannot be significantly improved. Local empowering action also requires a 'doing' state. If the state and NGOs can work together, then the strengths of one can compensate for the weaknesses of the other.

In the four countries under focus here, the overall relations between NGOs and state have been at least neutral and even favourable to the presence of NGOs. The Rural Support Programmes of Pakistan have sought and succeeded in drawing government resources into its own programmes. The Women's Centre for Change, Penang has managed to influence the government at project and policy level, and succeeded in bringing about certain critical legal changes in the system. Satyodaya in Sri Lanka wishes for government intervention and support to reduce ethnic tensions and to reduce the constraints faced by the marginalised poor. All the NGOs however are clear that while they may be doing some work in certain areas, they cannot have an overview of the overall needs of the whole society, which is the role of the state. What these NGOs are doing is trying to ensure in small ways that the interests of the disadvantaged groups are represented in and addressed by governments. Even when working in largely varying contexts, with extreme diversities, they all wish to enhance the responsiveness of government services to the needs of the vulnerable. These studies thus provide us with certain experiences, which make us reflect and broaden our perspective on the relationship between NGOs and the state.

DIFFERENT FORMS

The story of the NGOs in Asia is one of transformation, expansion and diversification. A major characteristic of NGOs in Asia in the early 1990s was their organisation at diverse levels of society. The sector is characterised by the co-existence of groups with different forms, goals and strategies. On a continuum of strategies, they take up developmental and service-oriented work; engage in policy advocacy in national politics; utilise lobbying, litigation and campaigning to reform the system; emphasise network, coalition and capacity building; and may be mass-based or staff or board-run. To secure financial resources, they have developed different ties and have also expressed their willingness to contribute resources from their own endowments—cash or labour, materials, knowledge, management skills and willingness to assume responsibility—in order to continue their programmes successfully.

The success of an NGO can be measured in several ways: through the extent of people's mobilisation, poverty alleviation, policy impact and cultural change, or that of change in collective consciousness and discursive politics. At the policy level, a major contribution to the women's movement has been the formulation of the Domestic Violence Act 1994 in Malaysia, through the sustained efforts of the Women's Centre for Change and other organisations. Malaysia became the first country in the South-East Asian region, and the first ever Muslim country, to have this kind of progressive legislation, and the WCC has achieved recognition as a participant in the making of the same. The recognition of domestic violence as a legitimate issue for public policy represents a triumph for the radical branch of feminism, which has defined this 'personal' issue as a political one. It has, thus, been able to obtain legislative intervention in family relationships by the state and that too, in a multi-religious, multi-ethnic society. Here NGOs have also demonstrated that service delivery and policy advocacy need not be contradictory or mutually exclusive goals.

In the official development discourse in the 1980s, issues of rural poverty and underdevelopment received scant attention. This was not because the incidence of poverty in Asian countries had declined, but because the priorities of the governments and the emphasis of many donor agencies lay elsewhere. Given this pervasive reality, the challenge was to bring forgotten issues back on the agenda. This is the great contribution of Rural Support Programmes in South Asia: they have drawn political and public attention back to poverty and development. They have also brought about other positive changes: the expansion of work and enlargement of goals, the diversification of programmes, efforts to recruit a new generation of social activists, and the development of new forms of people's representation.

Other clear trends emerge from these case studies. A decline in anti-statism, leading to more professionalisation and entry into governmental and political institutions, is evident in all the four projects described. The emergence and survival at the local level of a multiplicity of new and small NGOs responding to social as well as ideological diversity, thus providing the basis for the work of organisations such as Sahayi. In the countries covered in this volume, the rollback of state social welfare provisions, along with the growth of NGOs endeavouring to meet basic needs and promote development, has had the unexpected impact for NGOs of increasing funds for their work. But as the welfare state has dwindled, this increased funding has been accompanied by increased demand for such NGO work. Thus, all South Asian countries have in common the need to raise funds, yet without compromising their democratic and social values; and to meet basic needs while at the same time maintaining a critical advocacy role. This is a difficult task, which shows no sign of getting easier.

The NGOs here have established the dispossessed or marginalised in a particular space—a domain where they can collectively care about themselves and others, and the means whereby they can exercise control over their surroundings. They have offered provisions which the people can identify with. But there are only a few organisations of this kind existing in Asian countries today. The people who became attached to, and involved with these NGOs did so as a matter of choice, as part of their needs and desires. The question for the NGOs today is whether or not the design of an income generation or poverty alleviation programme, or literacy scheme can, over time, make people the 'owners' of the programme, so that they can eventually run it without the support of an outside agency. This is not to say that processes of empowerment through the NGOs do not aid the people. It is, rather, to suggest the need to evaluate the work of NGOs in different ways. The criteria for evaluation of empowerment should be less open-ended. Qualitative measures like 'creating awareness', 'gaining respect and acknowledgement', 'promoting understanding' and 'conscientisation' need to be supported by corresponding quantitative ones as well.

These are four organisations among thousands of others, and in only four of the countries in Asia. Their accounts do not by any means exhaust all the possibilities of what further explorations on this topic may reveal. They also do not lead to any tidy summaries or conclusions. What they show is that defining and exploring the practical details of empowerment, *matters*. More significantly, they also make us realise that organisations can only assist in empowering people, for real empowerment comes only with 'self-empowerment', when people can stake claim over power that is, in any case, rightfully theirs. For the individuals, it is a question of their life and survival, and much more than making a living. As for the collectivity, it is a question of whether just, equal and democratic civil life is possible. The need is to learn from

these four organisations, and many more like them, which continually
and tirelessly struggle with these questions.

NOTES

1. For details, see Joanna Rowlands, *Questioning Empowerment: Working with
   Women in Honduras* (Oxford: Oxfam Publications, 1997).
2. Naila Kabeer, *Reversed Realities: Gender Hierarchies in Development Thought*
   (London: Verso, 1994), p. 230.
3. Paulo Freire, *Pedagogy of the Oppressed* (New York: Seabury, 1973).
4. J. Clark, *Democratising Development: The Role of Voluntary Organisations* (London: Earthscan, 1991), p. 75.
5. D.C. Korten, *Getting to the 21st Century: Voluntary Action and the Global Agenda*
   (West Hartford, Conn: Kumarian), p. 207.

SELECT BIBLIOGRAPHY

Adams, R. *Self-Help, Social Work and Empowerment* (Basingstoke: Macmillan, 1990).

Afshar, Haleh (ed). *Women and Empowerment: Illustrations from the Third World* (London: Macmillan, 1998).

Barnes, B. *The Nature of Power* (London: Polity Press, 1988).

Dale, Ann and **John B. Robinson.** *Achieving Sustainable Development* (Vancouver: UBC Press, 1996).

Friedmann, John. *Empowerment: The Politics of Alternative Development* (London: Blackwell, 1992).

Giugni, Marco, Doug McAdam and Charles Tilly (eds). *How Social Movements Matter* (Minneapolis: University of Minnesota Press, 1999).

Grillo, R.D. and **R.L. Stirrat** (eds). *Discourses of Development* (New York: Berg, 1997).

Haynes, Jeff. *Democracy and Civil Society in the Third World: Politics and New Political Movements* (London: Polity Press, 1997).

Kaufman, Michael and Haroldo Dilla Alfonso (eds). *Community Power and Grassroots Democracy: The Transformation of Social Life* (London: Zed Books, 1997).

Khan, Mahmood Hasan. *Climbing the Development Ladder with NGO Support: Experiences of Rural People in Pakistan* (Karachi: Oxford University Press, 1998).

Radtke, H. L. and **H. J. Stam** (eds). *Power/Gender: Social Relations in Theory and Practice* (London: Sage Publications, 1994).

Wuyts, M. M. Mackintosh and **T. Hewitt** (eds). *Development Policy and Public Action* (Oxford: Oxford University Press, 1992).

Index

About the Foundation, Editor and Contributors

The Commonwealth Foundation is an intergovernmental organisation that promotes people-to-people interaction and collaboration throughout its 54 member countries. It supports NGOs, professional associations and arts and cultural activities through inter-country networking, training, capacity-building and information and cultural exchange. The Foundation gives priority to 'South–South' co-operation and activities that focus on poverty eradication, sustainable development, NGO/government relations and the strengthening of civil society. The Foundation has published several important documents including *Non-Governmental Organisations: Guidelines for Good Policy and Practice* (1995), *Spitting in the Wind: Lessons in Empowerment from the Caribbean* (2000) and *Reviving Democracy: Citizens at the Heart of Governance*.

Mukul Sharma is a Delhi-based journalist and writer, active in media and communications, voluntary organisations, trade unions and social movements. He has been writing on developmental issues in both English and Hindi for more than 20 years and has published numerous books and booklets, including *Against the Stream: India's Economic Crisis and Workers Alternatives* (1992) and *Landscape and Lives: Environmental Despatches on Rural India* (2001). He has received several prestigious national and international awards and fellowships for his writings on environment and on labour, rural, human rights and media issues. Sharma was a special correspondent of the *Navbharat Times*, New Delhi, till 1998 and was also the editor of *Labour File and Shramjivi* from 1995–1999.

THE CONTRIBUTORS

Ali Dastgeer completed his Masters degree from the London School of Economics in 1994. He worked in Pakistan for 7 years till 2002 where he headed the monitoring, evaluation and planning sections of the Aga Khan Rural Support Programme, the Sarhad Rural Support Programme and the National Rural Support Programme and was responsible for establishing the monitoring and evaluation (M&E) section at the Punjab Rural Support Programme. He was also instrumental in establishing the

RSP Network where he became the M&E Specialist. Dastgeer currently works as a freelance consultant.

Siti Hawa Ali is a qualified social worker who is currently teaching at the School of Health Sciences, Universiti Sains Malaysia. She has been a member of the Women's Centre for Change since its inception. She has held various positions in the organisation, including those of president, vice-president and secretary. She was also responsible for the development of the service section of the organisation. Currently she is a life member. She has also researched and published extensively on various related topics such as voluntary organisations and social welfare policy issues.

Gregory Placid hails from a village in Kollam district, Kerala, India. He has a Masters degree in economics and a diploma in adult and continuing education. He started voluntary work in 1972, and became a full-time social activist with Sahayi in 1990 where he has worked in different capacities, such as teacher, trainer, facilitator and co-ordinator. Presently, he is the Executive Director of Sahayi. Placid has authored several research papers and has actively participated in important national and international conferences.

Muthuvadivoo Sinnathamby is an Associate Professor of economics at the University of Peradeniya in Sri Lanka. He obtained his postgraduate degree from the University of Manchester, UK. His commitment to the welfare of the plantation workers in the country motivated him to work with NGOs and trade unions among these workers. For the past 20 years, he has devoted almost all his spare time to these activities. Much of his research and publications are related to plantation agriculture and labour. He is also widely experienced in evaluating the work of NGOs in Sri Lanka. He has represented the Ceylon Workers Congress (a union with the largest membership among plantation workers) in the Employees Trust Fund Board for several years. Sinnathamby has also served as consultant to a number of international organisations.